A Blue Coat Boy

in the 1920s

by

Danny Ross

Danny Ross.

A Blue Coat Boy
ISBN 0 9525543 5 6

First Published in 1996 by Pharaoh Press, Roby, L36

Typeset, printed and bound by
NEMO
Liverpool, L3 4BD

A Blue Coat Boy

in the 1920s

by

Danny Ross

Acknowledgements

For the opening of this story, 'A Brief History of the Blue Coat School, my thanks are due to the former Headmaster, Mr G.G. Watcyn B.A., who came to teach at the School as a Resident Master about 1926 during my time in the institution.

He was appointed Headmaster in 1945 and upon his retirement in the mid-sixties, he wrote and published 'A History of the Liverpool Blue Coat School – Past and Present' and it is from the records of his account I have been able to complete my first chapter.

D.Ross

Introduction

Although more than one history of the Blue Coat School and its founding have been written and recorded there has not been anything published about the day-to-day life in the School experienced by its inmates.

To the best of my knowledge and belief, this narrative is probably the only one ever to be written. It might not have been but for the inquiring minds of my children and grandchildren, who, over the years constantly questioned me about my life in the Blue Coat. They listened open-mouthed and with seeming disbelief – particularly on the question of food and the time for retiring at night and the early rising in the morning.

It was my dear wife who eventually persuaded me to record for posterity my schoolboy experiences, and so, for many years, I have been noting down events as I remembered them. It is possible there may be one or two little inaccuracies, but none serious enough to make any difference to my story.

1
The Liverpool Blue Coat School A Brief History from 1708 to 1920

The School was founded in the year 1708 by one Captain Bryan Blundell, a master mariner engaged in 'foreign trade' and the then Rector of Liverpool, one Robert Styth.

According to its history, the first School was organised by the Reverend Styth, who with public support, approached the Common Council with a request for "a convenient piece of ground for building a school for teaching poor children to read, write and cast accounts," and to be instructed in the "principles and doctrines of the Established Church."

Financial support was also necessary and here Captain Blundell's assistance was invaluable, for not only did he contribute the wherewithal for the first building, he did a great deal to secure subscriptions form the good citizens of Liverpool towards the maintenance of the School. The land on which the School was built was at the rear of St Peter's Church right in the centre of the town. A building which still stands today and is now owned by the Blue Coat Society of Arts.

Rector Styth died in 1713 and it is written that his loss was very keenly felt by Bryan Blundell who decided to give up the sea and undertake the care and running of the School, and the following year was elected Treasurer and Trustee in Robert Styth's place.

He very soon realised that the attendance at School by the children was being undermined by the poverty and ignorance of the times, and that out of school hours, the children got into "*such habits of idleness and met with so many diversions that they either neglect school or profit little by attending.*"

So Captain Blundell decided to convert it into a boarding school where the poor little boys and girls could be provided with "meat, drink, clothes and lodging" and where they could be kept "under such discipline and with the blessing of God might provide the desired effect".

So once more he set himself to raise funds towards the cost of extending the School buildings, and again the Council and good citizens of Liverpool did not disappoint, the council consenting to the extension and the citizens giving him the necessary financial support "*on the strength of which I went to work and got the charity school built which cost two to three thousand pounds, and was finished in 1718, at which time I gave for the encouragement of the charity, seven hundred and fifty pounds, being a tenth of what it pleased God to bless me with, and did then purpose to continue to give the same proportion of whatsoever He should indulge me with in the time to come, for the benefit and encouragement of the said charity*".

At first the boarders numbered about fifty, and by 1739 had increased to forty-six boys and sixteen girls. The numbers rose steadily in the following years and by 1742 there were seventy children in the school. In 1756 Bryan Blundell died and was succeeded by his son, Richard, who held office for only four years, and on his death his younger brother Jonathan became Treasurer and held office until near the end of the century by which time the number of boarders had risen to 375 pupils.

It was during the last years of the century that uniforms were introduced for the boys and girls, and were considered very smart and distinctive for the era, the boys being dressed in dark blue swallow-tail coats adorned with five silvery metal buttons over a dark blue waist-coat with five similar but smaller buttons, long dark blue trousers and black boots and a dark blue knitted cap. Tied around the neck was worn a white starched neckband similar to the ones used by the judiciary.

The girls wore long dark blue dresses, black hose and elastic sided boots and a white starched tippet worn over the shoulders folding down back and front and shaped to a point: at the base of the chest and the small of the back, crowned with a white straw bonnet fastened with dark blue ribbon in a bow under the chin. These uniforms were not to change over the years and continued to be worn into the twentieth century. The Blue Coat School continued to thrive and played an important part in the educational life of the City, and became a foundation earning the respect and affection of the townspeople of Liverpool.

It was realised however that the School buildings were inadequate, and it was in 1899 the Trustees accepted the advisability of removing the children to a new building on the then outskirts of the town in the Wavertree district, and the cost of erecting a new building was estimated at £80,000.

Thanks mainly to one Trustee, Mr. W. H. Shirley, who on his death in 1901 had devoted the whole of his fortune to the School which benefited from his Will to the extent of £38,000. This sum, together with many other donations, and the proceeds of the sale of the old buildings enabled the new premises to be erected in Wavertree. The present assembly hall, the Shirley Hall was so named in his memory.

On August 5th, 1903, the sixteenth Earl of Derby laid the foundation stone. The building was completed in 1906 and the children were moved into it in May of that year. Then on the 12th June, the Lord Bishop of Liverpool inaugurated it in company with Colonel Blundell-Holinshead-Blundell, a direct descendant of Bryan Blundell, one of the Founders.

It was into this School I was accepted along with my sister in July 1924 at which time there were approximately 200 boys and 100 girls Some true orphans but all fatherless.

2
My Introduction to the Blue Coat School

I was born in Everton, Liverpool, not of wealthy parents, fifteen months before the first world war broke out. My father by trade was a ship's painter, and as such was in a reserved occupation during the war camouflaging merchant ships and Royal Naval vessels in the dry docks of Liverpool.

I remember little of my early childhood but I do recall the small rolls of tracing paper brought home from work by my father, and when unrolled revealed the colouring plans of the vessels to be camouflaged. Some of the rolls were blank so I had plenty of spare paper on which to copy the outlines of the ships, and so kept myself interested and amused.

When the war ended however work was hard to come by owing to the deep after-war depression and money earned during the war and saved for a rainy day was soon spent and I remember my father in those early after-war years having to walk daily to the dock-yards looking for work which was either temporary or non-existent.

His health suffered being out in all weathers either walking to and from his work-place in heavy rain getting soaked to the skin, or at work itself being strung over a ship's side painting from a cradle, and the strong vapours of the lead paint blamed later for getting on to his chest and into his lungs.

He did possess an umbrella but only for use on Sundays and special occasions, and when questioned by my mother as to why he would not take his brolly to work, would reply "Don't be silly, how could any self-respecting workman go to work at the docks carrying an umbrella?"

"Very well," she would reply, "just see who is silly when illness catches up with you."

As time went on he became very 'chesty' and after a visit to a doctor chronic bronchitis was diagnosed. It was during the last months of 1923 his condition worsened, and he became confined to his bed for weeks at a time. I doubt if there were any anti-biotics or such for use in those days or he may have pulled through. He was a heavy smoker too which no doubt went against him.

His condition deteriorated, turning to pleurisy and pneumonia, and his doctor could do no more for him, and so he passed away peacefully on 26th January 1924. At which time I was ten and a half years old and the eldest of six children, the youngest two being twin boys.

My mother was distraught: and I became a great help to her by going messages to the shops and assisting to the best of my ability doing little jobs around the house, but for mother, life was very hard and the financial struggle became so critical she had to eventually bury her pride and appeal to the local Board of Guardians for assistance. She was advised to put my sister who was nine years of age, with me into a children's home, and that would be two less for Parish relief to support.

The Blue Coat School was recommended and my mother was told that this way two of her children would be fed, clothed and educated free, leaving her to manage at home with the four younger children for whom she would receive benefit. My heart went cold at the thought of leaving home, and up to then the only Blue Coat I had known of was the one my mother wore to go to church on Sundays.

Although the School in Wavertree was only about four miles from Everton, it might well have been on the other side of the world and I felt my future was not to be a happy one. Application was subsequently made to the Blue Coat and at an appointed time Mary and I appeared before the Headmaster, the Matron, and a small panel of Trustees in the School boardroom.

Apparently three of the required qualifications for admittance were that a child must reside within a ten mile radius of the Liverpool town hall, must be orphaned or fatherless, and should be of the Protestant faith as the School was dedicated to instructing all children in the doctrines of the Established Church.

After answering a few questions and reading out loud to the satisfaction of the panel, we were told to wait outside to be eventually told we were both accepted as prospective scholars and my mother who was present at the sitting was advised we would receive an admission date on which to report within the next month.

And so it was that one day in July 1924, Mary and I, accompanied by our mother, presented ourselves for admission. We were parted almost immediately, the new girls being taken into one room, and the new boys led into another. After a bath we all changed into School clothing which for me being on the small side, was a dark blue jersey, dark blue shorts, a cotton shirt and black boots and stockings.

The bigger boys were dressed in the School's recognised old fashioned uniform of dark blue swallow tail coat with silvery metal buttons, a waistcoat, long dark blue trousers and black boots and stockings. When we were all ready, our mothers were let into the room, and I can still hear the Headmaster saying "Now boys, say goodbye to your mothers," and still see my mother with tears in her eyes holding the small case into which she put my home clothes which I had just discarded.

Our gooodbyes were not long but very tearful and then we were led away by the Head into the precincts of the School, while no doubt the new girls were being led by the Matron to the girls' side of the School.

The time by now was mid-morning and dependant on age we were introduced into one of the five forms. I found myself in the third form, the Master in charge being Mr. Morgan, a Welshman, who as time went on I found to be very kindly though strict and a very good housemaster. At noon precisely class was brought to a halt and all the boys made their way quietly from the classroom and along the corridors. I sought the company of the other new boys in my class and together we followed the crowd out into the schoolyard.

We were there only a couple of minutes when a bell was tolled nearby and we were lost in wonderment as the boys lined up quickly and smartly into what we would learn later was 'table' order, ready to be marched to the dining hall for dinner. Each 'table' had its monitor (the word prefect was never used). There were four tables of boys lined up from the smallest on table one to the biggest on table four, and we new boys were latched on to the end of table four.

The duty master appeared as if from nowhere and on the nod from him we heard the command "Table one, left turn, quick march", followed by identical commands from the monitors of tables two, three and four. The march took us back into the building the same way as we had come out finishing up in the class-room corridor in one long column of two lines. At ten-past twelve another bell sounded from the kitchen area and the two boys at the front of the column opened first the double doors leading to the dining hall and then the doors of the dining hall itself.

Then came the order from table one monitor "Table one, quick march" followed by tables two, three and four. The dining hall was very large and I remember thinking it was the largest room in which I had ever been. It was very light and airy with large windows on one side and a very high ceiling. There were six long refectory tables (each made up of three smaller tables) made long enough for up to twenty two children to sit along each side.

The tables were covered with white linen table cloths, and had been set ready for eating. At each place was a dessertspoon, side plate upon which was a half round of dry bread and a small piece of cheese and a mug of water. The column of boys marched down each side of the long tables, and marked time by their place until the monitor shouted "Halt, left turn", followed by the same commands from the other tables.

All stood perfectly still at attention, while we new boys were falling about in disarray wondering why we had not joined the army instead. The girls meanwhile were filling up their two long tables having ambled in rather than marched. The duty master took up a position between tables three and four where there was a small table bearing a gavel and block. Grace was said by a boy before and after every meal. He had detached himself from the marching column on the way into the hall and stood ready to say grace at the master's small table near the gavel and block.

Amid complete silence the master tapped the gavel on the

block whereupon the boy stepped on to a small stool and said the grace, at the end of which was a loud "Amen" from the boys and girls. Another tap of the gavel and all boys and girls drew up their forms to the table and sat down on them in one combined clockwork movement, sitting perfectly still waiting for the next tap of the gavel which when it came a second or two later signalled the start of the meal.

Six maids – all civilian and employed in the kitchens – came through the dining hall doors and took up a position at the end of each table where already a huge tureen of hot, sweetened rice pudding had been placed. Each maid then took a plate from a pile stacked by the tureen and ladled a helping of pudding into it and passed it to the boy sitting at the end of one side of the table who in turn passed it on to the next boy and then it was passed on hand by hand down the table until it finally reached the boy at the far end.

This action was carried out alternatively down each side of the table until all had been served, and the maids returned to the kitchens.

I was sitting near the end of table four among the big boys, but facing towards the girls so I could pick out my sister across the hall. She too was facing my way and our eyes eventually met but we could only exchange smiles as talking or even waving was strictly forbidden. In fact all meals were taken in total silence, and it was a relief sometimes to hear the clatter of cutlery on dishes.

As well as a master on duty there was also a mistress. They

alternated in standing still and walking about the hall quietly, and occasionally one or the other of them strayed over to the other's territory and had a quiet word or two. At the end of the meal when the master had satisfied himself all had finished, back to the small table he went. A tap with the gavel and the boys and girls pushed away their forms from the table and stood to attention while the boy to say the after-grace made his way to the master's side.

A tap with the gavel and the-after grace was said at the end of which was a loud "Amen" and we were ready to be marched out. Table four first and table one last. Dinner had lasted about twenty minutes or so and we were marched out into the playground.

Being Wednesday we learned, the afternoon would be free. Classes were held on Saturday mornings in lieu of Wednesday afternoons. This particular afternoon would not all be free as we all had to be sized up and every boy in the school given a new number. So, about mid-afternoon we were all paraded in table order in the playroom which in actual fact meant size order as the smallest boy in the school was numbered one, and the next smallest number two and so on up the tallest boy in the school who could be numbered perhaps two hundred depending.

We new boys were slotted into the ranks according to our size, and all masters including the deputy head who took charge of this operation were present for the sizing up, each one being in possession of a large ruler or narrow length of wood. Each master was to size up about forty boys who were stood back to back, two at a time, the ruler being placed on the crown of their heads to see who was the bigger and so placed in size order.

At last the task was completed and starting with the smallest shouting number one, each boy shouted out his new number in turn right up to the tallest boy and this new number lasted for three moths until the next intake of new boys which was a quarterly event.

On two sides of the playroom row upon row of wooden lockers were affixed to the walls, and each one was approximately 15"x12"x12" and they were all numbered from one up to two hundred and twenty. After dismissal, all the masters except the duty master went away to their quarters, and each boy emptied his locker and transferred the contents to his new one.

The contents usually consisted of small games, books and perhaps boys' weekly papers and all the boot brushes and if lucky a tin of boot polish as well. Considering the lockers did not have any locks and could not be secured it was a credit to the boys that pilfering was seldom if ever encountered.

By now, it was approaching tea-time and we just about had time to go and wash our hands before being paraded in table order and marched to the dining hall. This time we new boys were in our rightful places, and my number was twelve and I sat at table one. We went through the same ritual for tea as for dinner, the marching in, the marking time, the duty master and his taps with the gavel and the grace. Our tea was nothing but a mug of hot milk, and one thick round of bread and margarine.

After the grace we all knelt down, and the boy who had said the after grace said, or rather intoned, the evening prayer. after the "Amen", we were all brought to attention with another tap from the gavel and marched out. My position on table one meant that I was sitting with my back to the girls, but I was much nearer and by occasionally turning round during a meal could catch my sister's eye and we could exchange smiles but that was all.

Back in the playroom we were dismissed and from then until bedtime we made our own amusement and could play games such as shoot, draughts or chess but being summertime we were all encouraged to go out into the fresh air in the playground. This was about eighty yards long and about thirty yards wide. At the near end under cover was the playshed while at the far end and down one side of the yard were iron railings about six feet high behind which were trees and shrubbery.

Down the other side was a brick wall topped with wide blocks of stone low enough to sit on and rest. Behind the wall the earth was banked up by about three feet to meet the level of the school playing field, which was about ninety yards square.

At seven-fifteen a bell was rung and all under the age of fourteen made our way back to the playroom but not before having a strip-down wash. At seven-thirty the duty master arrived and blew his whistle and all fell in this time in dormitory order, and we new boys not yet being 'housed' were stood to one side and we were eventually divided up into three small groups, each group then being put into a House.

There were three main dormitories or houses, Blundell House, Shirley House and Graham House or more commonly known as Lower One, Lower Two and Upper One respectively, Blundell and Shirley Houses being on the first floor, and Graham House on the second floor.

It must be said that there were three other dormitories, one large but un-named and known as Upper Two and only used about once per year when perhaps influenza took over and the sick bay full, and two smaller dormitories, one of which was called Lower Three catering for the over fourteens, and Upper Three which housed the poor unfortunates who were regular bed-wetters. These boys received medication and most were cured of the affliction in time and moved hack to their own House dormitory to which they belonged.

I found myself a member of Shirley House, Lower Two. Before we were allowed into the dormitories we had to change our footwear from boots to slippers or pumps. We ambled upstairs to the dorms rather than being marched, and I being small was in the front of the Shirley House column of boys, and as the dormitory doors were opened I was met with a vision I will remember to my dying day.

The beautifully polished floor receding about fifty yards into the distance with beds on either side the whole length of the dormitory with the reflection of the beds with their coloured cotton counterpanes on the highly polished floor was indeed a picture and made a lasting impression on my memory.

As we entered the dormitory we new boys were taken aside by the monitor, one Jim Hitchmough, and shown to our beds at the far end. The beds had already been made for us and upon inspection were complete with a mattress, two white sheets, two dark brown blankets and topped by a coloured counterpane or bedspread, and a white pillow with a long cotton nightshirt folded up underneath. We all had to stand to attention at the foot of our beds waiting for the orders, as we soon learned we went to bed by numbers, one to five.

On the command 'one' we shuffled as quietly and as orderly as possible to the toilet positioned half way down the dorm to relieve ourselves, after which it was back to the foot of the bed. On command 'two', we smaller boys took off our jerseys and folded them neatly on the chair beside the bed, the bigger boys taking off their coats and waistcoats and hanging them on the chairback, and all of us removing our slippers and putting them under the chair, and then laying our nightshirt across the bed ready to be donned, then back to the foot of the bed.

On the command 'three', we knelt by our bed and were expected to say our prayers silently, after which it was yet again back to the foot of the bed. When Jim Hitchmough shouted 'four', we undressed completely and folded our clothes and put them neatly on the chair, put on our nightshirts and finally jumped into bed. Any talking had to be done in whispers and anyone caught could be reported and punished.

After a few minutes the duty master entered and it was usual for him to walk the length of the dormitory to ensure all were safely a-bed, and satisfied walked back to the door and waited while the monitor shouted the last command – 'five' and we all chorused "Goodnight, sir" and on the reply "Goodnight, boys", he closed the door and went away to do repeats in the other dormitories. It must be noted here that during the darker evenings it was the duty master's responsibility to ensure all lights were switched off. We got our heads down for the night and silence reigned supreme.

As I closed my eyes and tried to catch my sleep I found it very difficult as so much had been crowded into the day, and I thought it is only about ten hours since I had said goodbye to my mother, but it seemed infinitely longer. The strong evening sun was shining in through the uncurtained windows and I very much felt like calling out to my friend a couple of beds away but knew I dare not break the silence.

For the first time since leaving home I felt very lonely especially as I thought of my sister and wondered how she was feeling away on the other side of the School, and of my mother and younger brothers at home. I confess I experienced homesickness for the first time in my life, and I am not ashamed to say there were a few tears shed before I eventually nodded off.

3
A Rude Awakening

It was indeed a very rude awakening the next morning at the unearthly hour of six o'clock. The loud bell in the School clock-tower had roused me from my slumber and it was still striking as I sat up quickly in bed almost in fright, and as that bell stopped another one started announcing the start of a new day. It was the same bell that was rung at meal times and as I learned later was situated in the kitchen area and was tolled every morning at six o'clock by a senior boy who rose a quarter of an hour earlier than the rest.

No one was allowed to sleep in and we quickly dressed, and instead of making our own beds as we usually would do each morning, being Thursday we folded our bed-clothes and stacked them neatly on the end of our beds with the sheets on top. Those sheets would be collected during the morning and taken away to the laundry for washing, and two clean sheets would be left in their place. I was surprised to find we were allowed to talk quietly while dressing etc., and when ready we made our own way downstairs to the playroom. There we polished our boots and changed into them putting our slippers in a space provided under the lockers.

Then it was along the corridors to the wash room to clean our teeth, have a strip down to the waist wash, brush and comb our hair then out on to the yard to talk and play. We each had a towel provided and each one numbered from one up and after use had to be hung on the peg provided with the same number, these numbers of course corresponding with our own personal number so that nobody could use that towel but ourselves. At seven o'clock we were paraded in table order and marched in to breakfast in the usual manner.

The first tap with the gavel had us all kneeling down while the boy who would be saying the graces intoned the morning prayer. After which grace was said and another gavel tap and we all sat down ready to start the meal. Thursday breakfast consisted of a bowl of bread and milk (nicknamed 'doffs') which we all ate with relish, but there was no more to be had and still hungry or not, after the grace was said we were all marched back to the playroom and dismissed.

There were two kinds of boys in the School - Band boys and Workers. The band boys went off to their practice in the bandroom to be conducted by the senior bandboy, while the workers made their way to the workers' place, which incidentally was right next to the bandroom, and they changed into their working clothes of old corduroy trousers and an old waistcoat and went about their chores. The younger boys filled in the time talking and playing games.

By eight-twenty band practice was over, the workers had finished their tasks and all were ready to be paraded and marched to the classrooms in time for lessons to commence at eight-thirty. Sometime during that morning we new boys were taken from our classes to the wardrobe room where we met the tailoress, Mrs Purvis, a widow who had a permanent position in the School, sewing, patching and mending our clothes.

The Head was also present while the tailoress took from the wardrobes some fairly new uniforms no doubt most of which were hand-me-downs from boys who had left the School, and so with some alterations needed which Mrs Purvis would attend to, we were fitted out with a best uniform to be worn for Chapel and Shirley Hall service on Sundays, and for other special occasions.

When we returned to the classrooms I was handed a letter from my mother, and told not to open it until we were dismissed at noon. It was a lovely letter and lovelier surprise to receive it so soon and when I eventually opened and read it I could have danced with joy. The good news was that she would be coming to take Mary and me home on the morning of the 20th, in nine days time, having been given this information by the Headmaster after saying goodbye to us on admission day. The reason being that the School was to be closed for a few days while the whole staff of masters and mistresses together with all the boys and girls went to the Wembley Exhibition. The news confirmed what we had heard from talk among the boys and which we thought may be a rumour.

Apparently the Wembley visit had been planned well in advance, we new boys and girls had not been included for which we were happier to be going home instead. Dinner that day consisted of one plateful of stew (called mash) and contained mashed potatoes, mixed vegetables and small pieces of meat and plenty of thin gravy. It was tasty but insufficient. We each had a mug of cold water too.

Afternoon class lasted from one-thirty to four o'clock with a ten minute recess half way through. Being Thursday we were due to drill between four and five o'clock, so after classes we all went out on to the yard to await Sergeant Major Porter from Upper Warwick Street barracks in Toxteth.

He always came in civilian clothes in spite of his title, and was a smart and disciplined soldier. Two boys from the band stood near the playshed, a bugler and a drummer. At a command from the S.M. the bugler blew the horn for the 'Fall In' – i.e. 'Fall In A', 'Fall In B', 'Fall In every company'. Upon which sound all 'fell in' in platoon order. There were four platoons. The new boys stood on one side of the parade until all were placed in a platoon. I was put in number three platoon. On the order 'Right Dress' the drummer played a roll on the drum until the S.M. shouted 'Eyes Front'.

Then the bugler and drummer laid down their instruments and joined their platoon. For the next hour we were "Right Dressing", "Numbering Off", "Forming Fours" and "Left and Right Turns" until we were dizzy and marching around while the old soldier bawled his orders until his waxed moustache bristled with pleasure. Dismissed at last, the S.M. went home for tea, and we went in for ours. This I found to be neither exciting nor sufficient, consisting only of one thick round of bread and marge and a mug of hot milk. The meal was soon over and we were marched back to the playroom and dismissed - but only for a short while.

At a few minutes to six the duty master appeared, blew his whistle and paraded us in table order and marched us up to Shirley Hall which was situated directly over the dining hall. It was indeed a beautiful hall with very large and long windows on either side making it very light and airy, and like the dining hall possessed a high ceiling. At one end of the hall was a platform at the back of which was housed a Willis organ proudly operated by the School organist Mr. Harling F.R.C.O. who incidentally also worked in the School office doing secretarial duties.

Not far from the platform and on either side of the hall were wooden forms banked up in terraces and it was into these forms we boys took our places – the smallest filling up the front rows and the bigger boys filling up the higher rows behind. When we were all seated one half of the boys were on one side of the hall while the other half were seated directly opposite facing each other. The girls meanwhile took up their places on forms between the boys in the centre of the hall, and for this singing practice faced the platform.

This practice gathering occurred twice a week, on Tuesdays between four and five o'clock. and on Thursdays between six and seven o'clock and always conducted by Mr. Harling. We each carried our own hymn books as supplied by the School containing hymns Ancient and Modern, anthems, and School prayers used in the Sunday afternoon services. We practiced the hymns chosen for the Chapel service the following Sunday morning, together with the hymns and anthems chosen fór the Shirley Hall service to be held the following Sunday afternoon.

These practices were something of a 'bind' to the boys and no doubt to the girls also, but they were of necessity and had to be borne with fortitude along with other rituals we did not like. Practice over we were returned to the playroom and had precious little time to ourselves as at seven-thirty found us going up to bed. Clean sheets had been distributed and our first duty on arriving in the dormitory was to make up our beds, and we new boys were given the necessary assistance and shown how it was done.

Once our beds were made, it was stand to attention at the foot and await the monitor's orders from one to five and we went through the same rigmarole as the evening before until it was at last 'Five' "Goodnight, sir" and we could all settle down for the night. We soon found out it was possible to smuggle a comic or boys' magazine to bed and in the light nights could snuggle partly under the bedclothes and read ourselves a bedtime story.

Strange to relate, this practice was seldom frowned upon by the monitors, but not openly encouraged either. I found it easier to go to sleep that second night and easier to rise the following morning when the clock-tower bell struck six. That bell, I should add, was silenced from nine o'clock at night until six o'clock in the morning. So it was jump out of bed, dress, make our beds and go downstairs to the playroom, clean our boots and put them on and then down to the washroom to complete our ablutions, then run into the morning air and play around until it was time to fall in and be marched to the dining hall.

Friday morning's breakfast was porridge ladled out by the kitchen maids and passed down each side of the tables hand by hand until all had been served. A mug of hot milk was also provided. I must mention that there were times when some porridge was still left in the tureens, and when this happened the maid stayed put a little while and this was the signal for some boys to swallow their porridge quickly in the hope of getting a second helping.

These boys then lifted up their empty places by just a few inches then tried to catch the eye of the monitor at the head of the table who at a nod of his head gave those boys permission to rise from the table and take their empty plates to the maid for some more. In this way quite a number received a second helping depending on how much porridge had been left in the tureen. For the record, this routine often happened when meals such as beans, mash, and rice pudding were on the menu.

After breakfast it was back to the playroom, and from memory I think it was a free day for the bandboys who did not have to practice every day, but the workers had no option and went about their allotted tasks as usual. Classes commenced at eight-thirty. Friday's dinner was baked beans served with a mixture of gravy and small pieces of meat, the meat being often fatty and nicknamed 'gizz' by the boys.

A mug of cold water was also served. For tea we had a bowl of doffs (bread and milk). After tea each Friday we received a bundle of clean undies brought in large basket from the laundry room. Each item in the bundle was numbered with the same number of course, and the bundle was tied up with a clean handkerchief also numbered.

My school number was twelve, and as I took my bundle it did not occur to me at the time that the boy who had been number twelve before me had worn these same clothes for the previous three months, and I would wear them for the next three months. Bath night was every Friday and the bathroom was positioned at the far end of the Shirley House dormitory, and contained about twenty five baths. Boys from Upper Three went in first, followed by the boys from Upper One, then Lower One, then Lower Two, and last to go in were the over-fourteens from Lower Three dormitory.

The end of Lower Two (Shirley House dormitory) nearest the bathroom was used as a changing room and where discarded dirty clothes were thrown into large laundry baskets as the boys ran naked into the bathroom where the duty master saw them into a bath, small boys two at a time, the bigger boys bathing singly. Each boy was given a towel to dry himself after which it was thrown into the laundry basket when they ran back into Lower Two before donning their clean nightshirts and slippers and going to their own dormitory.

Consequently with all this going on we Shirley House boys found ourselves getting to bed about an hour or so later than usual.

4
The Residential Teaching Staff

The Headmaster was Mr. H. C. Hughes who was a widower and lived with his grown-up daughter in quarters between the School office and sick bay. He was a tall and austere gentleman of the old school type, very sober minded and a strict disciplinarian who rarely smiled. I eventually found him to be a very kindly and sympathetic person who carried out his Headmaster duties to perfection, and he was very sadly missed when after a short illness he passed away in 1926.

The deputy head and senior housemaster was Mr. Chynoweth, known to the boys as 'Shinny,' a bachelor Cornishman. He was a first class mathematician and in charge of the top form. He was also sports master and took charge of the football and cricket teams. In private life he was a member of the Liverpool Cue-

fellows' club and was a first class billiards player. He could be seen on club nights dressed very smartly in a long dark overcoat with black velvet collar, white silk scarf, a silk top-hat and walking stick, unlocking a back door and letting himself out to a waiting taxi.

Shinny will be remembered for a most peculiar habit of raising his right knee while at the same time flicking the top of his right ear with the middle finger of his right hand, then bringing his right hand down quickly and slapping his right thigh. He was a very popular member of staff and was admired and respected by all.

Mr. Scott took charge of the second top class. He was the French master and taught the subject to the top two classes. He was a strict disciplinarian and a master to be reckoned with if one crossed his path. He left us early in 1926 to take up a position at a public school in the Lake district, and was never seen or heard of again, not by the boys anyway.

Mr. Morgan, a Welshman, was in charge of the third form. A very good housemaster and well liked by the boys, and it was a sad day when he too, found another school in his beloved Wales.

Yet another Welshman, Mr. Williams was master in charge of the second form. He too was very popular and unlike the others often came into the playground and pitched in with us playing football or cricket, and loved nothing better than to take hold of a bat and swipe a ball away to the far end of the yard with a habit of holding the bat in the air at the end of the stroke until the ball fell to the ground, then soaked up our admiration. He was another who was very sadly missed when he called it a day and left us in 1927.

Form One was made up of the youngest boys, ages eight and nine. They were taught by a non-resident teacher, a Mrs. Jones, who only served in the School from eight-thirty until four o'clock and never took part in any of the other School activities.

There was one other Master, Mr. W. Humphreys who was in charge of woodwork and handicraft. His classroom was the woodwork shop itself where he seemed to spend most of his time, even when not giving instruction. Woodwork was in our curriculum but we only had one lesson per week. 'Bill Humphs', as he was known to the boys, could be a grumpy old gent but was quite popular, and took his turn of duty master once every four weeks with the others.

All the masters were resident and had their own bed-sitters, and shared a large lounge between them which was comfortably equipped with small tables and easy chairs. Mr. Chynoweth had his own bed-sitter and a lounge to himself.

The duty week of the masters lasted from Sunday to Saturday night, and included all parading to and from meals etc. as well as attendance during meals and all activities after classes finished. They usually had one evening free during the week when Mr. Chynoweth always stood in for them by arrangement.

Nurse Taylor must have been about forty years old when I first became acquainted with her. She too, was residential and had her own living quarters next to the sickbay. It is worth mentioning here that the official name – probably by very long tradition – for the sick bay was the Nursery. For some unknown reason it was nick-named 'knock' by the boys. No one in my time could tell me why it was called this and no one could even guess or make up a reason. When a boy reported sick and had to be taken into the Nursery for attention he was referred to as "being up in knock".

Nurse Taylor was very officious, businesslike and efficient, but her manner at times could be frightening, especially to the younger boys who had to report sick with minor ailments. It is true that there were times when boys would rather suffer in silence with ear-ache etc., rather than go to the surgery for treatment. She did not like malingerers and lost no time in telling them so. Nurse held surgery every morning at eight o'clock - except Sunday - and any boy reporting for treatment was considered to have something really wrong with him.

Although my story tells the tales mainly of the boys' side of the School, I should include the Matron. Miss Rose Phillips was the most matronly of matrons one could ever wish to meet. Although in the prime of her life during my time in the School she was a lovely looking lady and must have been very pretty in her earlier years. She always appeared so clean and smartly dressed, her stiffly starched snow-white headdress, collars and cuffs worn to perfection, and her bearing and lady-like manner could never be outclassed.

We all saw Matron most days when she would breeze into the dining hall during a meal. She would come in to a chorus of "Good morning, Matron" or "Good evening, Matron" and in so saying we would all rise two or three inches from our seats in respect. She would sweep around the tables with a question here and there or passing some remark, but she was never known to ask "Have you had enough?" She probably knew she would be embarrassed by the answers.

Mr. Ernie Lynes is worth a mention, and was known disrespectfully perhaps by the boys as 'Liney'. He was a non-resident and served the School as its engineer. His main duty was being in charge of the boiler room which was next to the laundry. His task was to keep the boilers going to ensure hot water at all times to serve the laundry, kitchens and the washrooms all over the building. Friday was his busiest day as he had to generate sufficient hot water for the weekly baths. In winter he had the added responsibility of keeping the central heating at a top temperature to feed all the pipes and radiators throughout the school. In addition he worked in the cobbler's shop and attended to the mending of our boots.

On reflection I think he must have been a very important member of staff.

5
Prayers and Graces

As one has read earlier, both morning and evening prayers were repeated daily in the dining hall, and I believe they should be set down and recorded.

The graces before and after every meal were said by a different boy each time. It had started with the tallest boy in the School and then working downwards in number order, all taking turn saying grace, until it came down to number one – the smallest boy, then referred back again to the tallest boy, and carrying on the cycle ad infinitum. The morning prayer which was intoned and used before breakfast was taken from the C of E Book of Common Prayer and with which a host of people will be quite familiar:-

"Prevent us 0 Lord in all our doings, with Thy most gracious favour, and further us with Thy continual help, chat in all our works begun, continued and ended in Thee, we may glorify Thy Holy Name, and finally by Thy mercy obtain everlasting life; through Jesus Christ our Lord, Amen."

The evening prayer intoned each day after tea and before we vacated the dining hall was thus:-

"Accept: we beseech Thee O Lord, our evening sacrifice of praise and thanks-giving, particularly for the blessings of this day, for Thy gracious protection and preservation, for Thy loving kindness to us; for the opportunities we have enjoyed, for the instruction and improvement of our minds, for all the comforts of this life, and for the hope of life everlasting, through Jesus Christ our Lord. Amen."

The graces before and after each meal could have been peculiar only to the Blue Coat School, as I have never heard them used anywhere else. The before-grace went;-

"We beseech Thee Holy Father, to sanctify these Thy creatures, to the nourishment of our bodies, and to feed our souls with Thy heavenly grace unto eternal life, through Jesus Christ our Lord. Amen".

And the after-grace;-

"Thanks be to Thy Holy Name O most merciful Father, for this present refreshment of our bodies, for our daily bread and for all Thy mercies conferred upon us from time to time, through Jesus Christ our Lord, Amen".

At one time during my life in the School, a new master had come to teach us and was carrying out his duties in the dining hall for the first time and one boy had been dared to speak the wrong words in the after grace. The dare was for him to say "For this *slight* refreshment of our bodies" believing the new master would not notice; but he did notice and the boy was reported to the Head and duly punished.

But the boy was undaunted, he had won his dare.

6
Food

There was no doubt in our minds that we could have been better fed. The food was admittedly plain and wholesome, but never sufficient to satisfy our hungry appetites.

No doubt in the minds of the authorities we were given enough to keep body and soul together, and the fact that we could still run around and look healthy and happy told them all they wanted to know.

The day-to-day weekly meals – which never varied – are set out here for the sake of posterity, telling the world what exactly we had to be thankful for in our institution days.

The reading would seemingly be more at home in a Charles Dicken's novel.

MONDAY

Breakfast	One thick round of bread and margarine and a mug of hot milk.
Dinner	One bowl of pea soup, a small piece of dry bread and a mug of water.
Tea	One thick round of bread spread with treacle (which soaked well into the bread as there was no margarine on it) and a mug of milky cocoa or hot milk.

TUESDAY

Breakfast	One plateful of porridge (possibly two if there was any over) and a mug of hot milk.
Dinner	One plateful of baked beans and gravy with small pieces of meat and a mug of cold water.
Tea	One bowl of bread and milk.

WEDNESDAY

Breakfast	One thick round of bread and margarine and a mug of hot milk.
Dinner	One plateful of rice pudding, a small piece of dry bread with a smaller piece of cheese and a mug of cold water.

Tea One thick round of bread and margarine and a mug of hot milk.

THURSDAY

Breakfast One bowl of bread and milk.

Dinner One plateful of stew and a mug of cold water.

Tea One thick round of bread and margarine and a mug of hot milk.

FRIDAY

Breakfast One plateful of porridge and a mug of hot milk.

Dinner One plateful of baked beans with gravy and small pieces of meat and a mug of cold water.

Tea One bowl of bread and milk.

SATURDAY

Breakfast One thick round of bread and margarine and a mug of hot milk or milky cocoa.

Dinner One bowl of pea soup, a small piece of dry bread and a mug of cold water.

Tea	One thick round of bread and margarine and a mug of hot milk or milky cocoa.

SUNDAY

Breakfast	One thick round of bread and margarine and a mug of hot milk.
Dinner	One plateful of boiled potatoes, meat and gravy (no vegetables) and a mug of cold water.
Tea	One thin round of bread and margarine and one thin round of bread and jam (once a month we had a piece of fruit cake) and a mug of tea.

This diet for me only varied on a few occasions, otherwise it was the same week in, week out. To be fair, it must be pointed out that the bigger boys on tables three and four found their round of bread cut a shade or two thicker than the smaller boys on tables one and two.

Also, there were times – particularly when I first went into the School – that beef dripping was spread on the bread instead of margarine, and about halfway through my time there the monthly piece of fruit cake was increased to every Sunday.

Once a year on Matron's birthday – which was the 23rd

October or November – we were given sausage and mash for dinner, and it was understood Matron bore the cost of the sausages as a gift to the boys and girls. Naturally, she always made a point of coming into the dining hall during that birthday treat and she was greeted with a chorus of "Happy birthday, Matron!" and she would make her way around the tables in her usual way asking if we were enjoying the sausages and were they nice etc. If we got the chance, we would thank her personally for the treat.

The only time I remember a couple of dinners changing would be in the spring or summer of 1926 or 1927. To our surprise one day, instead of receiving our usual dinner, we were given a plateful of stewed rhubarb. Being very thinly made (the rhubarb, not us!) nearly everyone received a second helping. We relished it and thoroughly enjoyed it because it was something very different.

The only disappointment was that it was served on its own, there was no custard. In fact, in all my years in the School we never once had custard or jelly, or blancmange, or cream cakes, or honey, or toast, or egg, or bacon ... the list is endless and I could go on filling up pages with lists of certain foods we never received. Anyway, the rhubarb came again that week, and twice more during the following week – then it stopped. We heard down the grapevine that tons more could be given free by the benefactor but the School authorities had to say no to more as they could not afford to buy the large amount of sugar needed to sweeten it. And that was the end of the rhubarb saga!

Being always hungry the thought of food was never far from our minds, and it was not surprising the odd little ditty that was composed now and again and sung with gusto during our playtime hours. I can remember three of those ditties – one of which the words were as follows and sung to the tune of the hymn 'Jerusalem the Golden'.

"Oh, dining hall, the blessed with milk and doffs, blest,
Beneath our fancy waistcoats a basin of doffs will rest,
Oh, Martha in mercy give usa great big basin full,
So that we do not starve, and so we may not grumble."

Martha was a serving maid.

Another one we used to sing was to that old Sankey and Moody hymn 'There is a Happy Land'.

"There is a dining room not far away,
Where we get nowt to eat three times a day,
Ham and eggs we never see, get no sugar in our tea,
Fat as tubs we'll never be, we'll fade away."

And the third ditty we usually sang around Christmas time to another Sankey and Moody hymn 'Come to the Saviour, Make no Delay'.

"Come to the Blue Coat make no delay
Three rounds of chuck and a plate of beans a day
If you come at Christmas you get a currant bun,
So come to the Blue Coat, come, come, come.

Joyful, joyful will our Christmas be,

Our mothers' come to see us from one till half past three,
And we hang Daddy Pearson on a Christmas tree,
So come to the Blue Coat, come.

Daddy Pearson was one of the masters.

7
My First Weekend

On my first weekend, I was surprised to discover there was no relaxation. I thought a little lie-in might be allowed on Saturday and Sunday mornings, but no, we were all up at six o'clock as usual, and after our early morning rituals were over and breakfast was finished, we all found ourselves back in the playroom or out in the yard.

There was no let-off for the workers either, they all had to attend to their tasks as usual on Saturday and we were all in our classrooms by eight-thirty, ready to start our lessons. We finished at noon and after dinner, the afternoon was our own. A School cricket-match was played, against which team I have forgotten, but I remember we lost by three wickets.

Boys not playing in the match watched from the sidelines on

the playing fields or joined in other games in the yard. I was surprised to see older boys in civilian clothes joining in the yard games and I learned they were old-blues who had left the School in recent times and were allowed to visit freely on Saturday afternoons. They were welcomed by their friends and more so perhaps, because they brought sweets and chocolate which were unobtainable to us there as there was no tuck shop.

After playing out all afternoon in the fresh air, I was ravenously hungry and looking forward to going in for tea, and hoping there would be something worthwhile going in for – so imagine my surprise and disappointment at sitting sown to one round of bread and marge and a mug of hot milky cocoa. After tea, the time until getting ready for bed was our own so I went to my locker and took out my mouth-organ. It had been given to me by a friend on coming into the Blue Coat as a 'going away' present. I could not play it properly and practised sucking and blowing in the best way I knew how, trying to play the latest pop tune of the day which was 'Ma, He's Making Eyes At Me.'

The tune came in time but the tinny sound of the single strained notes coming out left a lot to be desired. And, as someone unkindly mentioned at the time "no wonder you can't make any friends". Even though it was Saturday, bedtime was no later and we went up to the dorms at the usual time. Sleep was not coming any easier and as I lay in bed I wondered what Sunday had in store. I expected my mother would be coming to the afternoon service in Shirley Hall as she had mentioned it in her letter, so when I awoke the following morning I had that to look forward to.

Sunday's activities were different. After our meagre breakfast time was ours to talk and read. Being the Sabbath day meant we could not play any outdoor games of any kind, and time in the playground was spent walking round and round in groups, chatting, or sitting on the low wall commonly known as the bank, talking with friends.

At ten o'clock, we were taken – one table load at a time, smallest first – to the wardrobe room to change into our Sunday best uniforms, and by ten forty-five, we were all lined up in size order in two ranks in the playroom corridor to be made ready to go to Chapel.

We were numbered off in pew order, so many boys to a pew and at two minutes to eleven were marched off the the School Chapel for morning service. There were two doors leading into the Chapel, and one half of our column containing the smaller boys waited outside one door, while the bigger half waited outside the other door. As the clock tower bell began to strike eleven, the Chapel doors were opened and we could hear the strains of the organ playing the School march.

The organist, Mr Harling, changed to slow time, and with four beats to the bar played the entrance march, and in we boys marched in twos in perfect time to our pews, which we slowly filled up the sides of the Chapel, followed in by the girls, also marching in slow time and they filled up the centre pews.

The service was conducted by the Chaplain of the School, one Canon Twitchet, who was also the vicar of Holy Trinity Church next to the School. Mr Chynoweth was also in attendance and sat at the front of the Chapel just below the pulpit, facing the bigger boys, while on the opposite side of the Chapel, facing the smaller boys, sat the duty mistress who had brought the girls to Chapel.

The morning service was as printed in the Book of Common Prayer of which we all had our copy so we could follow the prayers and sing the canticles, such as 'Te Deum' and the 'Jubilate' etc. When the time came we all recited the Apostles Creed together, and of course sang the accompanying hymns we had practised earlier in the week, and listened to the lessons and the sermon with some interest.

When the service was ended it was around mid-day, the Chaplain departed and we were all slow marched out, girls first, and were marched straight to the dining hall for dinner. The meal of boiled potatoes, meat and gravy was quite tasty and enjoyable, but like all the other meals, there were no afters.

Again after dinner we were not allowed to play games, so we passed our spare time either walking around the yard or talking and reading in the playroom until a quarter to three.

At that hour the duty master appeared and blew his whistle which was the signal for us to line up again in the corridor as we had done for Chapel earlier. We were numbered off in what was our seating order and then marched to Shirley Hall for the afternoon service. At three o'clock the two entrance doors were opened and we could hear the strains of a voluntary being played on the organ by Mr Harling.

At a nod from Mr Chynoweth who had accompanied us to Shirley Hall, the organist gave four slow beats to the bar and began to play the slow march and we all marched in slowly with heads erect, keeping perfect time, and took up our places on each side of the hall.

The girls followed us in slowly and took up their places on forms in the centre of the hall, facing the congregation made up of guests, visitors and old boys and old girls of the School who came regularly each week. The visiting mothers and relations of the boys and girls tucked themselves up in the gallery, from where they could pick out their children more clearly. The service itself was so unique that I have decided it is worth a special mention and it is described fully later. Two of the Trustees were also in attendance.

The service consisted of an opening and closing hymn, two anthems sung choir-like by the boys and girls, questions and answers on the Catechism, prayers were said and concluded with the Lord's Prayer, after which came the closing hymn.

We all slow-marched out of Shirley Hall, but not before paying our respects to the two Trustees, the boys bowing and the girls curtseying on the way out. We all made our way then down to the dining hall below where our teas were already set out by the kitchen staff. We boys marched in and took our places at tables, followed by the girls, and once grace was said, we started our meal, which looked inviting with the red jam on the top round of bread and a mug of tea.

The door on the girl's side of the hall was opened. The space between the girls' tables and the side of the hall under the windows was roped off, creating a passage about twelve feet wide, and into this passage the mothers, friends and other visitors crowded and made their way slowly through the dining hall, filing out at the far end. For us, this was the happiest times of the afternoon, being able to smile at our mothers and wave to them discreetly, but there was a long tradition – no talking.

It took only a minute or two for the mothers to pass by and it was sad to mouth a bye-bye to them as they disappeared through the far door. I soon bucked-up however remembering my mother would be coming to take me and my sister home the following Saturday.

Tea finished and the after-grace said, but we did not have the usual evening prayer as we had just said prayers in Shirley hall. Back to the playroom we went, and the time being only about four-fifteen we had plenty of it on our hands in which to read, talk or play quiet board games on the playroom table. Our next assembly came at six forty-five when we all lined up in table order in two ranks facing each other this time.

Two senior boys had come from the kitchen carrying between them a large box and passed it down the ranks. The box contained nearly two hundred pieces of dry currant bread, each one measuring about 3"×2"×2". Each boy was allowed to take one piece only – and this was our supper – only given on Sundays when our tea was always an hour or so earlier. That 'currant bango' as it was called, tasted delicious, and an hour later our weekend was over and we were all tucked up safely in bed.

8
Shirley Hall Service

On marching into Shirley Hall, a boy detailed to read the prayers detached himself from the marching column and made his way to the pulpit positioned in front of the platform and organ, behind the girls and naturally facing the congregation.

We could not start the service without the presence of the two Trustees, the Headmaster and the boy Catechist. They came in from the opposite end of the Hall, walked down the aisle and the Trustees took their places on throne-like chairs positioned just in front of the congregation. The Head sat right behind them on a chair raised slightly higher so that he could easily be seen giving signals at appropriate times. The boy Catechist stood at the Head's left side.

The organist was still playing a melody up to this point, but once the Trustees and Head were seated, he stopped. The service would be conducted by the boys and girls, no-one else participating except Mr Harling on the organ. To commence the service, the Head nodded to the boy in the pulpit who opened by saying, "Let us sing to the praise and glory of God, hymn number so and so," and then uttered the first line of the hymn.

All joined in the singing, and when it ended, the Headmaster, by holding out his hands in a certain position, made a sign at which all the boys and girls knelt down, and at a nod from the Head the prayer boy read a couple of evening prayers taken from the book of Common Prayer. After which, another sign, and the boys and girls stood up. Then a prayer boy announced, "Let us sing to the praise and Glory of God an anthem", and read out the anthem's first line. The anthem was sung only by the children just like a massed choir, the congregation listening in awe as the singing was so beautiful.

At the finish of the anthem and at another signal from the Headmaster, all the children sat down except those taking part in the Catechism. usually an average of twenty boys and sixteen girls took part, all came to the front and lined up in a vacant space in front of the Trustees forming three sides of a rectangle, ten boys down one side, the girls across the back or second side, and the other ten boys down the third side.

The Catechist took up his position in the centre facing the first boy to be questioned and at a nod from the Headmaster asked the first question, "How many sacraments hath Christ ordained in His

Church?" and the boy answered, "Two only, as generally necessary to salvation, that is to say Baptism and the Supper of the Lord".

Then the Catechist asked questions in turn to all the other boys and girls, the answers being most interesting and informative. The questions all finished, the Catechist stepped back a pace or two, and immediately facing the Trustees, and was joined by a boy on his one side and a girl on his other, both of whom had been chosen by the Head to recite the lessons, one each from the Old and New Testaments.

When the lessons were finished, the Catechist took one step forward and both he and the other boy bowed to the trustees while the girl curtsied. Then, at a signal from the Head, all the boys and girls returned to their seats. Another anthem was sung, and more prayers read, ending with one which I have never forgotten.

"Bless this and all other schools for religious and truly Christian education and direct and prosper all pious endeavours for the propagation of thy gospel in the world. These praises and prayers we humbly offer up to thy divine Majesty through the mediation of they Son, Jesus Christ our Lord, in whose most holy name we sum up all our desires ..."

The Lord's Prayer followed this, recited by everyone in the Hall. After the final hymn, we all slow-marched out and down to the dining room as described in the last chapter.

It was often said in later years by those having taken part in, or witnessed that weekly service that television came too late to record the event for posterity. The boys and girls dressed in their eighteenth century uniforms, and the novelty of the service conducted by the children themselves, whose ages ranged from eight to fifteen years for the boys and up to sixteen for the girls, surely must have made a wonderful documentary.

The questions and answers on the Catechism were taken from an official Church publication, based on Baptism, the Lord's Supper, the Apostle's Creed and the Lord's Prayer. Two sets of questions and answers on Baptism, two sets on the Lord's Supper and one each on the Creed and Lord's Prayer. They were all included in the Shirley Hall services and repeated every six weeks. Boys and girls were selected to take part in the weekly Catechism, the girls by the Matron or senior mistress, and the boys by the Head or his deputy. Rehearsals were held through the week and again on Sundays immediately after dinner.

I remember when I was asked to take part for the first time and was set to answer the first question which happened to be on Baptism. The Catechist asked, "What is your name?" and when I replied, "Daniel", the Head chipped in saying, "Oh, Daniel, come to Judgement", giving us one of his rare smiles. As time went on and I got a little older, I found myself being introduced more and more into the Catechism, reading the prayers and eventually taking a turn at reciting the lessons.

In the dining hall after the service we were always joined by the two Trustees, the Headmaster and Matron. It was a tradition that the Head took one Trustee to the boy who had recited the lesson and the boy was congratulated and given a shilling, while the Matron took the other Trustee to the girl who had recited her lesson and she too was congratulated and given a shilling.

On special occasions such as Remembrance Sunday and Old Blues Sunday, Shirley Hall was packed to capacity, and on these occasions, Mr Harling always took the opportunity of changing from the School march to 'Land of Hope and Glory' while we slow-marched our way out and the sound of our marching feet on the wooden floor reverberated loudly through the Hall and, the tune arousing some dormant patriotism within us, we puffed out our chests and held our heads even higher.

On these special Sundays, it was not unknown for the Trustees on duty to give the boy and girl who had recited the lessons a ten-shilling note!

9
Getting Acclimatised

For me, the following week could not go fast enough, but it ended at last, and on the Saturday we new boys and girls left to go home for a few days while the rest of the School children were driven away in tramcars to Lime Street station, en-route to London and the Wembley Exhibition.

The holiday at home passed all too quickly, and I confess to feeling very dommy (homesick) on my return to School where there was great excitement and many stories to relate from the boys who had been at Wembley.

I soon settled down again and gradually found the weekly pattern of activities seldom varied. I have set them down here for you.

Monday	Classes morning and afternoon Drill in the yard between four and five o'clock
Tuesday	Classes morning and afternoon Hymn and anthem singing practice in Shirley Hall between four and five o'clock
Wednesday	Classes morning, afternoon free Playing out in the yard or School field
Thursday	Classes morning and afternoon Drill in the yard between four and five o'clock and after tea, hymn and anthem singing practice
Friday	Classes morning and afternoon Bath night – starting at about six forty-five
Saturday	Classes morning, afternoon free Playing out in the yard or School field
Sunday	Chapel service in the morning Shirley Hall service in the afternoon

The next happy occasion to look forward to was Sports Day, which would take place about the middle of August. Some of the more agile, enthusiastic and athletic types were allowed onto the playing field, running, jumping and training for the big day. Most of us, however, chose to spend our time in other quieter and less strenuous ways. On one occasion, I was passing my time away playing my mouth-organ, when a boy about my own age and size came over and said, "Hey, Ross, that's not the right way to play the thing, come with me and I'll show you the proper way to play it and I'll give you a few tips at the same time."

I went with him to his locker from which he took a double-sided mouth-organ which must have cost all of one shilling and eleven pence. He played a tune for me and didn't he play well! To use an old-fashioned expression he could make it talk, although of course, he was no Larry Adler. After some tips, guidance and encouragement from him, and a whole lot of practising holding my mouth and tongue correctly, I was very pleased to find I could make music from my mouth-organ sound a lot easier on the ear.

I felt rather flattered later when Alf, the boy who had taught me, invited me to play a duet with him. As time went by, Alf and I grew more friendlier and a true friendship blossomed which was to last all through our life together at the School.

I would have liked to join the School band but knowing next to nothing about music I hesitated in asking. When I did pluck up the courage and asked Mr Chynoweth about the possibility, he questioned me on music and my knowledge of brass instruments. Unfortunately, I could not answer satisfactorily and he told me enthusiasm was not enough and that in his opinion I would make a very good worker. So that was one ambition squashed in its infancy.

He told me boys' names were added to the list of workers when they reached the age of twelve, and that was something I could look forward to with some fear and apprehension. There was a saying used often in the School – "Workers are workers and band boys are shirkers". The School premises of course had to be kept clean, and bringing in outside cleaners would have been too expensive for a charity school, so it had been a tradition from time immemorial that boys and girls should be used to keep everywhere clean and tidy by brushing and dusting, polishing and ... scrubbing!

Excluding the band boys and the young ones under the age of twelve, that left approximately eighty to a hundred boys who could be called upon to work. Quite a large army of workers – but they were all used to cover the daily morning tasks of brushing and dusting the main corridors, sweeping the washroom floor before it was washed or scrubbed out, cleaning the wash-bowls and polishing the brass taps and pipework, scrubbing out the latrines and cleaning and swilling out the urinals, and brushing and dusting the classrooms.

Upstairs, the dormitories were dusted and brushed before the wooden floors were waxed and polished. The four oldest and therefore senior workers stayed out of class nearly every morning on alternate weeks, two one week and two the next, and were officially known as 'stayers out'. Their work started at eight-thirty in the morning when all boys were in the classrooms and the corridors were clear, and their work consisted of scrubbing the marble stone floors of the corridors from end to end on Monday, Wednesday and Friday mornings – first the classroom corridor, the washroom corridor and then the playroom corridor.

On Tuesday, Thursday and Saturday mornings, they worked upstairs, scrubbing the marble stone floors on the first and second floors leading to the dorms, as well as cleaning out and scrubbing the five dormitory toilets, cleaning the baths and scrubbing the bathroom floor.

Thankfully, none of this was for me yet as I had the best part of a year until my twelfth birthday, but it gave me plenty of food for thought.

Sports Day was not far away now and a lot of the more enthusiastic types spent most of their spare time running round the playing field and timing their laps etc. Some were given the apparatus to practice hurdling and jumping. Nearer the day, the senior monitors of each House were invited by the sports master, Mr Chynoweth, to submit the names of the competitors for the main events, together with the names of the boys who would be competing in the novelty events, the latter boys being less athletic.

Then came the eliminating rounds of those competing in the track races and some practice for the boys competing in the novelty races, such as the boat and chariot races. As Sports Day drew nearer, so did the excitement, for our mothers would be automatically invited and we could look forward to spending an hour or so with them after the races were completed.

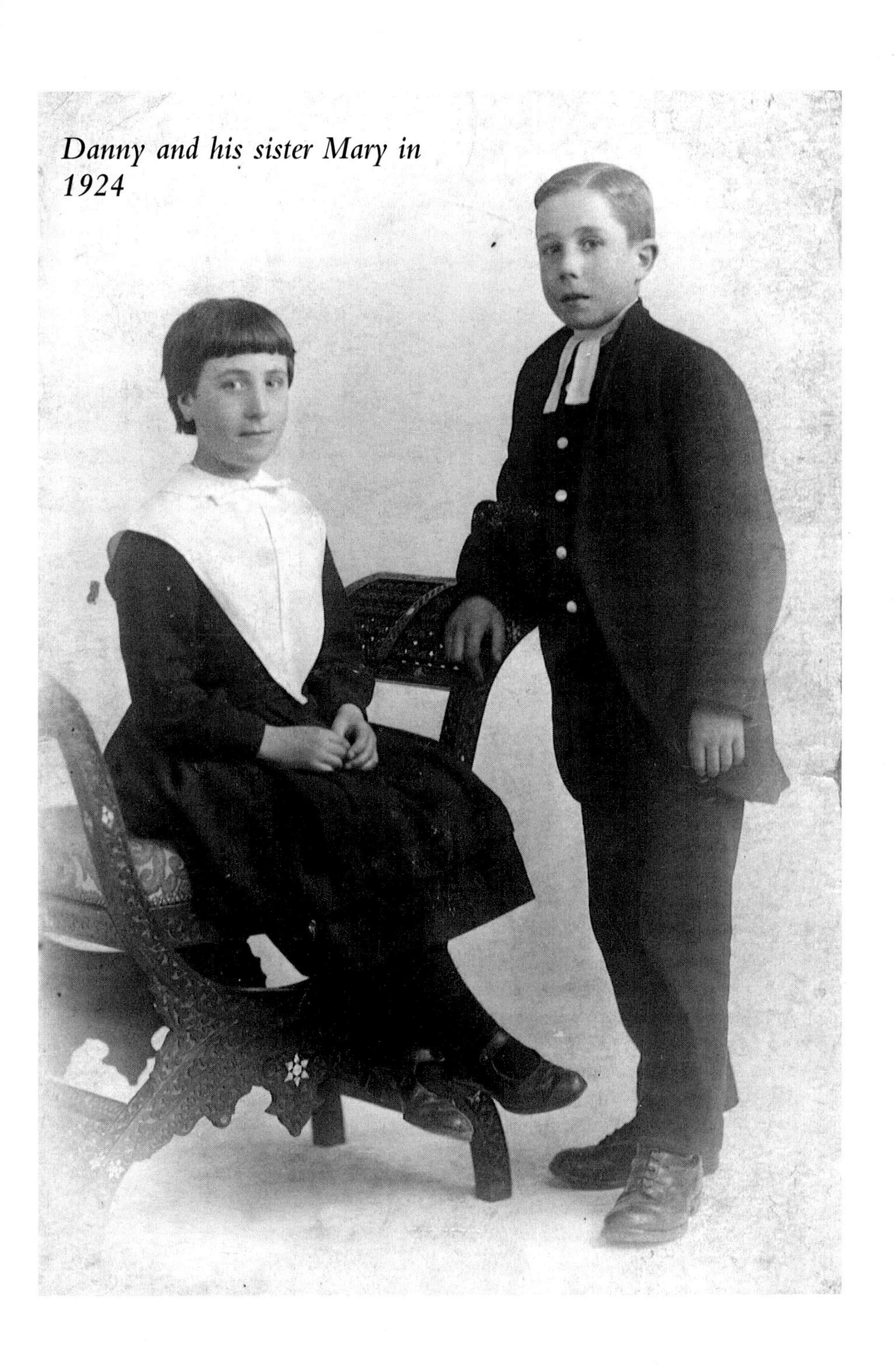

Danny and his sister Mary in 1924

The Blue Coat School Wavertree

The Dining Hall

The School Band

Shirley Hall

Boys' Drill Squad

A group of boys enjoy the sun in July 1927. Alf Lennon is sitting second from right in the middle row

10
High Days & Holidays

There were a small number of 'high days' we experienced during the year, mainly in the summer months. First Prize Day coupled with Drill Inspection; the annual trip by sea from Liverpool to Llandudno and Anglesey as guests of the Liverpool and North Wales Shipping Company; Sports Day and of course, our School holidays when we were allowed to go home to mother for three weeks and three days in May and the same in September.

Ten days holiday were granted at Christmas but spent in the School, and Christmas Day itself was very special. At Easter time and Whitsuntide we were given the usual bank holidays as well as one in August, but more about these later.

Sports Day finally arrived and the events would commence early in the afternoon. During the morning, boys were excused classes and detailed to carry chairs and benches from many parts of the School to the playing field, under the supervision, and at the direction of a couple of masters, and they were placed in rows one one side of the ground ready to receive the invited VIP's and guests.

Benches and chairs were also placed on what we called 'top field' for our mothers and their friends, at right angles to the VIP's but with an extra good view of the events. Meanwhile, the sports master put the finishing touches to the layout of the 'Field' ensuring the starting lines and the finishing posts and tapes were all in order and that all the apparatus etc needed for the novelty races were there and in position.

Just before two o'clock, we boys were led onto the field and took up our cheering positions on the opposite side to the guests, while the girls were assembled in an area to the left of the guests. The main field events for the boys and girls were the flat races of 100, 220 and 440 yards, the 100 yard hurdle race and the high jump and the long jump.

Points were awarded for these events, three for the winner, two for the second and one for the third. Any boy or girl could compete for the maximum points and the one who collected the most was declared the 'Victor Ludorum' and held the silver cup for the next twelve months.

While the track events created all the excitement, the novelty races aroused more fun and laughter, especially the chariot race. Five boys from each House made up the chariot, two big boys in front with an arm around the other's waist, two other boys crouched behind with backs bent low and their hands grasping the arms of the ones in front, the smallest boy then climbed up and stood on the backs of the two who were crouched down behind the jockey and grasped the reins tied to the arms of the leading two boys.

It was apparently quite easy for the jockey to stand up straight while the chariot was in a stationary position, but as soon as the whistle blew to move off and race a hundred yards which included a couple of bends, he found the jogging soon put him off balance and tumbles were frequent and caused much laughter among the spectators.

Another novelty was the boat race. Here, each house fielded a team of seven boys and a cox. The boat was a length of timber about sixteen feet long and three inches square. Each 'boat' was painted in its House colours – red for Shirley, blue for Blundell and green for Graham – and laid out out at the starting point about six feet apart.

The seven crew straddled the length of the boat with legs apart facing the cox. When the whistle blew for the start of the race, each boy would lift the boat up between his legs and start running backwards towards the winning post a hundred yards away. The cox had the job of steering the boat by shouting orders to the crew such as "a little to the left," or "more to the right" as well as trying to keep the crew in step. Trip-ups were many, as may well be imagined, and caused much merriment to the onlookers.

There were other fun-giving races such as the obstacle race, plant pot race, sack race, egg and spoon race, tug of war and finishing with the pillow fight where contestants tried to knock each other off a polished pole. All excellent fun creating plenty of excitement and happiness. The day ended with the silver cups and prizes being presented by the Lady President of the School Ladies Committee, after which all the special guests were escorted into the Boardroom for tea and biscuits, while we boys and girls spent the rest of te afternoon on the playing field with our mothers.

Saying goodbye to them an hour or so later was not too difficult for we knew that in three weeks time we would be going home for the September hols. After tea, most boys were put to work clearing the field of chairs and benches and carrying them back to their respective rooms, and all the sports equipment put back into cupboards for another year. The boys did not hurry as the longer they took the later they would go to bed.

Time dragged by for the next three weeks and the first Monday in September could not come quick enough for the holidays to begin. On the last Sunday of term, the boys and girls looked forward to singing their favourite hymn at the close of the afternoon service in Shirley Hall, N° 577 in the Ancient and Modern hymnbook, 'Lord dismiss us with thy blessing'.

Then, at about six o'clock we were all assembled again in the Shirley Hall to be addressed by the Headmaster and the Matron.

We were warned as to how to conduct ourselves during the holidays by being well-mannered and properly dressed. Every grown-up we spoke to or were approached by we must address them as "Sir" or "Madam" and we must be polite and well-behaved at all times, and show every respect, particularly to our elders. The short assembly closed with both the Head and Matron wishing us happy holidays.

No-one minded getting up at six o'clock the following morning, and after breakfast we were all ushered out into the playyard with our bags packed, having emptied our lockers the previous evening. We lined up along the bank below the playing field in size order, higher numbers at the head of the queue and all led by the Catechist who was regarded as head-boy, and the monitors.

On the stroke of eight o'clock from the bell in the clock tower, it was a very happy line of boys who made their way up the steps to the top field and then along the front of the building to the main entrance, where the Headmaster and the Matron were waiting on the front steps. They shook our hands individually and bade us goodbye and again wished us a happy holiday. The we found our mothers in the waiting crowd and went off home on a tramcar.

11
Autumn

Again, our holidays at home passed all too quickly, and I confess I was not enjoying the prospect of returning to School to face a long confinement. Over seven months would pass before we wold be allowed home again, so we had the long autumn and winter months to look forward to, perhaps with some interest but certainly with some apprehension.

We always returned from holidays on Wednesdays and could expect to see our mothers again the following Sunday at the Shirley Hall afternoon service, and afterwards see them walking through the dining hall while we had our tea.

Chapel service preceded that of course, at eleven o'clock in the morning, the first hymn being N° 576, the one we all liked least of all, 'Lord behold us with thy Blessing'. It was never sung with gusto but only with a feeling of depression and serving to confirm the fact that we must resign ourselves once again to almost prisoner status.

Our day-to-day lives seldom varied, nor did the food, except for the sausage and mash on Matron's birthday, and I was told Christmas dinner would be special. Approximately once every two months we were taken out of School for a walk on Wednesday afternoons. It meant us having an extra wash after dinner then off to the wardrobes to change into our best uniforms before parading in the yard in table order.

When the duty master considered us ready to move off, he took charge of tables one and two, say, while another master took charge of the other two. Out of School we were marched, but once out of the gates the two parties split-up, one going down Penny Lane and on to Sefton park, and the other perhaps to Woolton Woods or Calderstones Park. We were allowed to amble along the main roads rather than march and we could talk amongst ourselves, but could not raise our voices in any way.

It was grand to be out on the street, walking amongst ordinary folk, even if it was only for a couple of hours, and our presence always created a passing interest to bystanders and shoppers. It was not unknown for some people to clap as we went by, nor was it unknown for some kind lady to run after us and press a bag of sweets into the hands of the lucky boy at the rear of the column.

For me, still a new boy, I enjoyed the walk tremendously and could not understand until I grew older why the longer serving boys would have preferred to spend the afternoon in School, playing football or other games. The walk was usually times for us to arrive back no later than four-fifteen, giving us plenty of time to change out of our best uniforms and be marched in for tea.

Trafalgar Day on 21st October was to be our next big occasion. The Trafalgar memorial in Liverpool stands in the centre of Exchange Flags immediately behind the Town Hall, and I learned an annual service of remembrance and wreath-laying ceremony took place at eleven o'clock on the morning of the day itself. We were excused lessons on that particular morning and, dressed in our best uniforms, were taken by tramcar into the city.

We were accompanied by the Headmaster and his deputy and two other masters. In charge of the parade however, was Sergeant Major Porter, our drill instructor, who looked very smart in his bowler hat and dark overcoat. We alighted from the trams by the Queen Victoria monument, where the SM lined us up in marching order with the School Brass Band in the lead.

On the order the band struck up with the march, 'Old Comrades' and we proudly marched in perfect step across the top of James Street and along Castle Street, to the cheering crowds, skirted the Town Hall and took up our position amongst the sailor lads assembling at the Trafalgar memorial.

It was by long tradition the Blue Coat School boys were invited, and we were the odd ones out being surrounded by all the different branches of the HM Naval units, officers and cadets from the training ship *Conway*, officers and boys from the able-seaman's ship, *Indefatigable* – both vessels being permanently anchored in the Mersey and boys from the Liverpool Seaman's orphanage. The town's Lord Mayor and other civil dignitaries were also in attendance.

After the short service and the laying of the wreaths, the salute was taken by the Mayor, and back we were marched to our tramcars to be taken back to School for a late dinner. It was my first experience of marching behind a brass band and I thoroughly enjoyed the thrill of it. In fact, the occasion left a deep and lasting impression on my mind.

As autumn wore on, the shadows lengthened and the clocks went back one hour and our games and pastimes became confined to the playroom. Board games and shoot were the most popular, while a few boys had fretsaw sets and busied themselves making models. Others chose a quiet space on the wide window-sills and read, with their legs and feet dangling over the warm radiators.

On Saturday mornings only, mothers were allowed to hand in at the main door parcels of fruit for their children, but sweets and other foodstuffs were forbidden. Two large linen baskets were placed in the porch, and parcels for boys placed in one and parcels for girls placed in the other. The baskets were taken during the afternoon to the boys' and girls' sides of the School and the parcels distributed after tea. The fruit was very acceptable as it was never included in our menus, and those fortunate enough to receive fruit shared it out amongst their friends, and it was surprising how long one could make a banana last.

My friend Alf was well-known for bringing song-sheets back from his holidays at home. He once told me that in the neighbourhood where he lived – which was in the Toxteth area of the town – an empty shop would be rented for a day or sometimes just an afternoon, by musically-minded business people who installed folding chairs and benches into the shop, together with a piano in the window. A smartly dressed sporty gentleman at the door took a small entrance fee and sold song-sheets a a penny or twopence a time. Meanwhile a lady pianist took her seat at the piano and began to play. Apparently, it was surprising how much interest was generated to fill the place up and how popular a sing-a-long could be. It was all quite similar to the song booths found in many seaside resorts.

Alf, in his Blue Coat uniform, was always welcomed and let in free and he enthusiastically joined in the singing and learned most of the latest popular songs by heart and so was able to sing them to us and play them on his mouth-organ.

Once every few Saturday evenings between six and seven o'clock depending on the whim of the duty master, we held and enjoyed impromptu concerts in the playroom. Tables and benches were pushed into one half of the room and we all sat, stood or straddled over them, hoping for a good viewing spec. Volunteer names had been given to the duty master who called them out to perform in the order of the programme he had drawn up.

The concert was most enjoyable and successful with us listening to recitations, the singing of little comic songs, some of which we all joined in as audience participation was encouraged, and Alf was always good for a tune on his mouth-organ and would sing some of the songs from his repertoire.

During the long evenings – I state they were long but they only seemed so, as from tea to getting ready for bed was only an hour and a half – when I was not engaged in playing draughts, dominoes or shoot, I whiled away the time reading adventure books or comics borrowed from friends and often consoled myself by having a go on my mouth-organ.

Watching boys playing chess fascinated me, not just the boys playing, but the game itself. Altogether I must have spent hours and hours watching and gradually – and very slowly – I picked up the moves of the various pieces and eventually learned what the game was all about. Once I started to play myself, I soon began to win the odd game against weaker opponents, and I knew I had realised an ambition and so played as often as possible, to improve.

Bonfire night was upon us and some boys expressed the hope of a repeat of a previous year when a master accidentally dropped a naked light into a box of fireworks. They say there was an almighty bang with coloured lights, sparks and rip-raps flying everywhere. I got the feeling that the more the story was told the more exaggerated it became. No-one had been injured but the show was over much earlier than anticipated.

For us, however, the firework display was to commence at six o'clock. We boys were all lined up standing along the bank skirting one side of the playing field, and the girls with the Matron and mistresses being assembled on a balcony outside the Shirley House dormitory in a raised position so they had a better view of events that we did.

The masters in charge of the display were in the centre of the field surrounded by boxes of fireworks. The joinery master had prepared a large wooden framework from which the fireworks – catherine wheels, smaller pinwheels, sky rockets and roman candles etc – could be dispensed. As they exploded, sending coloured flares flying into the air, the cheering of the boys and girls knew no bounds and the hour or so passed all too quickly. A good time was had by all and after the show was over we went in and to bed with the strong smell of cordite filling our nostrils.

I realise I have mentioned little of the academic side of the School in affecting our young lives. We were given to understand that the Blue Coat School was considered to be a cut above the ordinary elementary schools in the city, being on a 'secondary' level. The only difference I noticed for my age, however, was that I was now being introduced to science and algebra which I had not done previously.

Otherwise I found myself holding my own when compared to others in my form. There were no GSE exams to worry about in those days, nor any 'A' levels. Examinations only occurred twice a year, once in December and again in June, and covered all the usual subjects in our curriculum. French was taught to the two top forms, so I had to wait until my second year to learn my first sentence in French and never will I forget it – "Nous sommes dans un grand batiment".

In my first couple of years in the School we did not have a morning assembly; that was to come later. Religious education was not given as a special subject, but every morning from eight-thirty to nine o'clock we sat in class studying our prayer books having to learn and memorize various sections which we were told would stand us in good stead when confirmation came along.

Confirmation reminds me of something I should have mentioned earlier. Every Sunday morning after breakfast and before we changed into our best uniforms to go to Chapel, we lined up in the wash-room and received a teaspoon of hair-oil from nurse and rubbed it into our hair. It did not smell very nice but it did put a shine where it was needed. We understood it to be coconut-oil.

On confirmation Sunday, boys about to be confirmed were not given any hair-oil as it 'might soil the hands of the Bishop', at the laying-on ceremony. Every boy and girl had to be confirmed when they reached the age of thirteen and special instruction was given to confirmation candidates in special classes after school hours.

Thinking back, no-one was asked if they wished to be confirmed, and many no doubt had been baptised into the Methodist, Congregational or other Free churches, but all in the Blue Coat School were confirmed in the Church of England. We were required to learn the Apostle's Creed, the Ten

Commandments, our Duty towards God and to our Neighbour, the Lord's Prayer and the 'Desire'. All these could be found in the first section of the Catechism in the Book of Common Prayer, which we had been strongly encouraged to study in our early morning sessions.

We were also taught to remember from our Shirley Hall service Catechism the following;

Question	How often is a person to be confirmed?
Answer	But once.
Question	Why not oftener?
Answer	Because the intention of it is to ratify the Covenant made at Baptism which can but once be administered.
Question	What happens when a person is confirmed?
Answer	The Bishop lays his hands upon the head of the person to be confirmed, and solemnly prays that God will give him grace to keep his resolution, and confirm and strengthen him in all virtue and goodness.

When confirmation day came, candidates were told it must be regarded as a red-letter day in their lives and should not be treated lightly. The actual service itself was quite short, being incorporated into our usual Sunday Morning Prayer. I can vouch for the fact that the solemnity, dignity an seriousness of the service and especially the laying-on of hands by the Lord Bishop made a lasting and profound impression on our young minds.

12
Winter & Spring

Next upon us was the season of Advent heralding the coming of Christmas, which for us, was one of the happiest times of the year. The lead-up was tantalisingly slow from that first Sunday in Advent by the gradual introduction over the next four weeks of the Christmas hymns and carols. As mentioned earlier, our holiday in School covered a ten day period , so from 23rd December until the New Year we were allowed to stay in bed until six-thirty! This was a bonus too for the resident masters and mistresses.

I am sure we all particularly enjoyed the singing of the carols, and as well as the more popular ones, there were others I had never heard of, before or since. In fact, I still sing three of them, or at least as much as I can remember, every Christmas, mostly to myself, as they still haunt my memory. I have, over the years, looked for them in different church hymnals, and at one time, even made enquiries in religious book-shops, but I was never able to trace them. I do believe they are worth putting on record.

"Now over the snow-white meadows in throbbing ebbs and swells, are sounding the happy voices of joyous sweet Christmas bells, Oh sweet is the strange wild music that floats o'er the listening earth, Oh sweet is that strange wild music that tells of a Saviour's birth.

Ring out wild bells and greet the morn
Proclaim the tidings Christ is born,
Ring on, ring on sweet Christmas bells".

"In the fields with their flocks abiding, they lay on the dewy ground, and hovering under the starlight the sheep lay white around, When the light of the Lord beamed over them and lo from the heavens above an angel leaned from the glory and sang his song of love.

He sang that first sweet Christmas, a carol that never shall cease, Glory to God in the highest, on earth goodwill and peace."

There are other verses to this carol, but my fading memory cannot recall them.

"Cradled all lowly behold a Saviour child,
A being holy in dwelling rude and wild,
Ne'er yet was regal state of monarch proud and great

Who grasped a nation's fate
So glorious as the manger bed of Bethlehem.

No longer sorrow as without hope O earth
A brighter morrow dawned with that infant's birth
Our sins were great and sore but these the Saviour bore
And God was wrath no more.
His own Son was the child now born in Bethlehem.

Babe weak and wailing in lowly village stall
Thy glory veiling, thou cam'st to die for all,
The sacrifice is done, the world's atonement won
And life its course hath run,
Oh Jesus Saviour morning star of Bethlehem."

I remember the tunes perfectly but unfortunately I cannot write music, so I regret to say I must end this portion of my story on an unsatisfactory note.

For the first time in my young life I did not hang my stocking up going to bed on Christmas Eve, and I thought, well, there had to be a first time, and here it is! Some boys though, did hang theirs up, just for a joke they said and were not too disappointed when you know who didn't come.

Christmas morning was just like any other Sunday morning to us. After our normal breakfast we had about three hours before Chapel, but could not go out to play, so it had to be a quiet morning indoors. As we slow-marched into Chapel later, I noticed the visitor's seats were filled more than usual with a lot of well-dressed ladies and gentlemen, who it transpired were the Trustees and their ladies, and there were also a lot of old boys and girls of the School in attendance on this special occasion.

The service was brighter than usual, made more so by the singing of carols, and the chaplain, Canon Twitchett, preached an inspiring and more interesting sermon than usual. The service over, we slow-marched out and were taken straight down to the dining hall followed by most of the visiting congregation.

For the twelve days of Christmas the dining hall was decorated with mistletoe and holly around the lights and windows and parts of the walls. Christmas dinner was our usual Sunday fare – meat, potato and gravy – but today, as well as being given a knife and fork, a dessert-spoon was set for every girl and boy.

The Trustees, their ladies and the old scholars came into the hall and were allowed to talk to us while we were eating. We too, were allowed to talk between ourselves, the only meal during the whole year we were allowed this privilege.

When we had finished the first course, the Headmaster introduced the Chairman of the Governors who made a short speech, wished us all a Merry Christmas and announced Christmas Pudding would now be served.

The centre dining hall doors were opened leading from the kitchens and in walked two Trustees carrying a big tray between them, on which large Christmas Puddings with steam rising from them were paraded around the hall while we boys and girls were allowed to cheer and bang our spoons on the table.

The din was terrific and I have since witnessed the piping in of the haggis but that was nothing by comparison. The puddings were shared out so many to a table, while six kitchen maids appeared to do the slicing up and passing of platefuls of pudding along the tables until we were all served.

We had been warned to eat carefully as many threpenny bits had been thrown into the puddings while being mixed. Second and third helpings seemed to be the order of the day there being so much pudding on offer, and as the old boys took our plates for that second or third helping they dropped threepenny pieces into the pudding on the way back. In later years, one old boy told me how he and others saved all the threepenny bits they could through the year for that special occasion.

Dinner over, all the guests and visitors left to go home and we were marched back to the playroom, dismissed and left to our own devices until about two o'clock when our mothers arrived and were escorted to us in the playroom. The re-union with them was very happy and they brought Christmas presents and fruit, sweets and chocolate – which we were allowed to eat on this day once a year! It was a day too, when boys who had sisters in the School could stroll over to the girls' playroom and mix freely, and of course the girls could wander over the boys' domain.

The afternoon passed all too quickly and happiness turned to sadness when the duty master blew his whistle on the proceedings and our mothers had to leave us with sad goodbyes. After they departed we toyed with our new presents until tea-time and again after tea until bed-time. It was my first Christmas away from home and apart from being locked up in the institution, the day had been happy, especially as I was able to share part of it with my mother and my sister.

The remainder of the Christmas holidays passed all too quickly, either playing football in the yard, or indoor games and reading in inclement weather, and before we realised it, we were wishing each other Happy New Year. We were always looking to the future and the next happy event. Mine would be 22nd January, my sister's birthday. It was a rule of the School that mothers could visit their children on their birthday, and if the mother had other children in the School as well, she could see them all together.

The mother had to report to the office at four o'clock in the afternoon on the birthday and after permission was given by the Head, the office boy or 'gate' boy was sent to bring the birthday child with any brothers or sisters to their mother waiting in the office. The family was then escorted to a meeting place just outside Shirley Hall where they could spend a happy hour together. It was hard luck on a boy or girl whose birthday fell during the May or September holidays, and they were not compensated in any way for losing out on a visit from mother.

Easter was next on our horizon. The winter months with dark mornings and evenings meant we were confined more indoors than playing out. Sometimes when the frost and ice were thick on the ground we made slides on the playground that were fifty or sixty yards long.

In the light of the dawn we ran and slid long distances to our great pleasure with never a thought as to how much damage we might do to the soles of our boots. When we went in to class at eight-thirty our hope was that the icy slides would not melt away in the morning sunshine, but they often did, much to our disappointment.

From time to time during the dark evenings we had visits from local amateur concert parties. The players gave freely of their time and talents as they entertained us on week-day evenings in the Shirley Hall. Those concerts brightened up our lives considerably and were most welcome, and as they seldom finished before eight-thirty it also meant us staying up an hour or so longer than usual, and that to us was an extra bonus.

When the weather was dry we still had our occasional walk on a Wednesday afternoon to a local park which kept us in touch with the outside world, of which we saw very little. Then, on one occasion, all of us boys and girls were invited by the management of a local cinema to the showing of a film called 'Charlie Chaplin in the Goldrush'. It was a silent film of course, as were all films in those days, but it was very funny indeed and provided the best laugh in a long time and the memory of it haunted us for a long time afterwards.

On some Saturday afternoons our first eleven played football matches against local opposition, which created a lot of interest and sporting entertainment when playing at home on the School playing field, but when they played away they took no support with them, because it was said, funds would not allow for the tram fares.

The season of Lent was soon upon us, although the forty days in the lead-up to Good Friday passed by very slowly. Looking back, we were never required or even taught to give anything up for the Lenten period, probably because they knew we had nothing to give up – save perhaps the reading of comics or boys' magazines etc. Life for us was sober enough as it was.

Good Friday itself was different though. It, with Easter Monday, constituted our holiday, so no classes. The workers however were required to do their stint on both days. Good Friday morning found us in the Chapel for an eleven o'clock service which was both sad and mournful.

After dinner, we changed out of our best uniforms into our every-day attire, From then until three o'clock – the ninth hour – we were expected to stay quiet and read or talk, as no games of any kind could be played. When the bell in the clock tower struck three the solemn 'watch' was over and we were then allowed to run about and play games. After tea, being Friday, we paraded in the usual order to the bathroom and had our weekly scrub-down.

Easter Saturday was as normal. However, Easter gifts of chocolate eggs and sweets were accepted in parcels as well as any weekly fruit parcel, so the office boy and gate boy were kept busy all day taking the parcels in from our mothers and putting them into the large baskets for boys or girls.

Fruit parcels had to be stowed away separately as they would be given out as normal that evening. The Easter egg parcels were kept until Easter Monday morning. On Easter Sunday we had a bright and happy morning service in the Chapel, and then the service in the Shirley Hall in the afternoon followed with our mothers and visitors filing through the dining hall as normal while we had our tea.

Easter Monday meant we were free all day. We were assembled in the playroom about ten o'clock and the large basket of Easter parcels was brought in and we each collected our parcel as our name was called. We were quickly dismissed by the duty master with the warning not to make ourselves sick!

It is worth recording that a large store in the city, McSymons by name (which has long since disappeared), presented the School each year with a very large chocolate egg about three feet high and about two feet wide. It was smashed into little pieces and we each received a piece of that chocolate egg at tea time on the Monday evening. I was told this tradition had been carried on for many years dating back no doubt to the time when McSymons' store in Church Street was a very near neighbour to the Blue Coat School in School Lane, before the boys and girls had been moved to their new premises in Wavertree.

13
Summer

The first monday in May was our next happy occasion to savour when we would be allowed to go home on holiday for three weeks and three days. The clocks had long been put forward which meant that somewhere we had lost an hour's sleep, but as someone commented at the time, "never mind, it's an hour nearer to our hols".

The lighter evenings did not mean a great deal to us as we still had to go to bed at seven-thirty and it was harder to catch our sleep. On the other hand it was a change to smuggle up a comic or boys' magazine and read a little under the bedclothes before dozing off.

Whispering to one's partner in the next bed was simple enough providing you were at the opposite end of the dormitory from the monitor, and 'I Spy' was often played in whispers without being caught out. For small offences such as talking or acting the goat on parade etc, a monitor had the power to tell a boy to "go and report yourself". The offending boy would then report himself to the duty master, even if it meant having to go to the masters' study to find him, and then a punishment would be meted out. The punishment was never really severe, more irritating, it being to "stand by the study for half an hour", or perhaps an hour, the study being that which belonged to the deputy Head, Mr Chynoweth, at the wardrobe end of the washroom corridor.

It was a common sight after every meal to see maybe half-a-dozen or more boys standing to attention outside the study by order of one or more masters for small offences committed during the course of the day. I must state however, while on the subject of punishment, be it standing by the study, or three or four of the best on the hands from the head or his deputy for more serious offences or writing lines in the classroom after lessons, there was never any physical cruelty or abuse during my five years at the School.

As usual, our Spring holiday at home went by far too quickly, and in no time at all we were back to the grind in School for another three months. Summer was now upon us and football had been left behind – cricket was now the order of the day. Chalk was borrowed from the classroom and the railings down one side of the schoolyard chalked up as wickets while bats and balls appeared as if from nowhere.

Whip and top was a popular pastime in those days, and many tops were being whipped up and down the yard by enthusiasts. Some boys were lucky enough to have their own roller skates and skated up and down, adding to the noise and confusion, while the quieter boys sat on the bank reading, talking or playing games.

Once we got back into our stride in the classroom, our examination papers in different subjects had to be tackled and took about ten days to complete. Meanwhile we were still being drilled twice a week by Sergeant Major Porter. Drill Inspection and Prize Day would soon be with us and was our next High Day, when our mothers were welcomed among the visitors.

This was the one day when the band boys came into their own and they had to suffer extra practice with the band master, Mr Harling. The bandroom echoed for days with the strains of the music to be played for the General Salute, the March Past and a piece called 'Evening Shadows' – which was to be played during the General's inspection.

Just before the day came, the smartest platoon – as nominated by the Sergeant Major – had been notified and each boy in that platoon could expect to receive a bright new shilling from the General on parade at the appointed time. Boys and girls who had done well and come top of the exams had also been notified they would be receiving a prize and were instructed as to when and how to act when the time came.

The great day at last with us, the band-boys were put through their final rehearsals after breakfast, while the workers set about their tasks, before lessons started at the usual time. Immediately after dinner the older and bigger boys helped with the seating arrangements for the visitors on the field, and then it was a quick change into our best uniforms with clean neck-bands being distributed. Just before two o'clock everything was ready for action, the girls had taken the field in an area left of the VIP's and guests, while we boys were paraded in platoon order onto the yard.

Promptly at two o'clock the band struck up and we marched proudly onto the field, responding smartly to the shouted orders from the Sergeant Major who marched us over to the far side of the field and positioned us ready for inspection by the General and his Aide de Campe. During the inspection of the ranks the band played 'Evening Shadows' and when it was over the General saluted the parade and strode back across the field to the saluting base ready for the march past.

This was done in platoon order with the Sergeant Major looking resplendent in his army uniform leading the way. Every Blue Coat boy who ever took part will surely remember his command "March past – advance in column – by the right quick march". The band immediately struck up with the tune while we all sang quietly to ourselves what to us where the accompanying words ...

"What did you join the army for,
Why did you join the army?
Oh what did you join the army for,

You must have been blooming well balmy."

As each platoon marched in turn past the saluting base, its commander shouted the order, "Eyes right!" and saluted the General, who in turn returned the salute.

When the march past was over, the smartest platoon – as mentioned earlier – were paraded in front of the VIP's and as each boy was ordered from the ranks by a signal from the SM, the drill was as follows. March smartly towards the General; halt two paces away from him; salute smartly with the right hand; take two paces forward; shake hands with the right hand; take the shilling with the left hand; take two paces backwards; salute smartly again; right about turn; march smartly back to your place in the platoon.

This was the final act of our drill and we were all marched across to the far side of the field and stood at ease. There followed a short dancing display by the girls to the strains of a piano, and when it was all over, the field was cleared and all the visitors and mothers were shepherded into the Shirley Hall.

Prize-giving was next on the agenda and by the time we boys and girls walked into the Hall, Governors and special guests – including the Lord Mayor and the Lady Mayoress – were assembled on the platform, while the remainder of the visitors took up the seats in the main body of the Hall. The mothers, as usual, filled up the balcony.

Short speeches of welcome were made by the Chairman of the Governors and the Headmaster, followed by a patriotic song, 'What heroes thou has bred, Oh England my country'.

accompanied on the organ by Mr Harling.

After this the prizes were distributed by the Lady Mayoress, and again those to receive a prize were instructed that on hearing their name called would walk across the front of the platform; stop by the Lady Mayoress; left turn; bow politely (or curtsey for the girls); take one pace forward; shake hands with the right hand; take the prize with the left hand; one pace backwards; another bow or curtsey; right turn and walk smartly off the other side of the platform.

Then followed a few words of congratulations to the prize winners from the Chairman, and commiserations to the rest with the hope we might do better next year, and the proceedings were brought to a close with the singing of the national anthem. We boys and girls were marched out and returned to our respective playrooms, while the special guests were treated to light refreshment in the boardroom, and the mothers were allowed to join us children for a happy hour or so in the playrooms. This re-union was for us the most enjoyable part of the day , and those boys who had a bright new shilling nestling in their pockets were, of course, happier still.

Very soon afterwards came the day of our annual trip to Beaumaris in Anglesey, the girls going on the Tuesday and the boys two days later. The band boys – lucky chaps – were invited on both trips, for they were expected to and did make music on the top deck of the ship, much to the delight of the crew and civilian passengers on board.

After breakfast on our appointed day, we changed into our best uniforms and were led out to the waiting tramcars and taken to the Liverpool Pier Head. Alighting from the trams we lined up in fours near the Royal Liver Buildings and with the School band playing a lively tune we marched down the floating roadway onto the landing stage and along to where the ship, *La Marguerite*, was berthed. It was a paddle steamer.

I had been told a tale by older boys that on a previous trip that when the vessel was about to leave Llandudno pier to go on to the Menai Straits, because all the passengers crowded onto the starboard side of the ship, waving to the people on the pier, the ship listed so much that the port side paddle wheel was above the waterline and could not be put into action.

As a result, the Captain bellowed through a loud hailer announcing the trouble and requesting half the passengers go over to the other side of the ship, and so set it on an even keel. The story went on that as they all wanted to see a paddle wheel sticking up out of the water they all moved over to the port side, whereupon the ship then listed to port and lifted the starboard paddle wheel above the waterline. The captain was said to be outraged because he could not get his ship underway until the crew had dispersed all the passengers.

I, and others like me, had swallowed the story hook, line and sinker, and wondered what might happen when *La Marguerite* arrived at Llandudno. Of course, nothing akin to it did happen, but it was a sailor's yarn I can never forget.

As you can imagine, our trip was a huge success, really fabulous with glorious weather, wonderful scenery and calm waters all the way. We were treated to tea and sandwiches down below, both on the outward and homeward journey. After landing the civilian passengers at Llandudno we went on to Anglesey and disembarked at Beaumaris pier. We were told we were on our own, to be well behaved and to be back in one hour to start the journey back home to Liverpool.

Boys who had been before led the way into the small town to a sweetshop in Castle Street where the owner was kept very busy selling one and twopenny bags of sweets. Then it was off to Beaumaris Castle where we were admitted free of charge, and had a great time exploring the place from top to bottom. That hour ashore vanished in what seemed like only ten minutes and, not wanting any trouble we all arrived back at the ship on time. Our voyage home was just as enjoyable, and when we got back in School we realised and acknowledged just how lucky we had been to have had such a happy day.

14
The First Year Over

By the middle of July I had to tell myself those first twelve months had not been as bad as I had anticipated. I realised it was only the first couple of months which had been the unhappiest when the feeling of homesickness had predominated. Since then, there had been four intakes of new boys in October, January, April and now July. I was beginning to feel like an old sweat having recently had my twelfth birthday and I had just been informed that my name had been added to the workers' list.

My first job was sweeping the open corridor which ran from the far end of the playroom corridor, along past the surgery, the cobbler's shop, on past the doors leading up to the office and the dining hall and along to the open back yard, on the opposite side of which were the boiler house and the laundry and an entrance to the kitchens.

The length of the open corridor was about seventy yards, and starting sweeping from the playroom end, I found it got much dustier and dirtier the further I swept, especially when I reached the back yard where it was open to the elements. The dirt, when collected into a heap, was shovelled into a bucket which was then carried to an area at the end of the yard which we called 'Piggy', where there were about half-a-dozen dustbins placed, and the bucket emptied into one of the bins.

A roadway from this open yard ran round to the front of the School on the main road near the Chapel. This roadway was known to us as 'Piggy Lane' and was used mainly by merchants delivering dairy and kitchen produce, and lorries bringing coal for the boiler house.

My job wasn't bad but with the workers' list having to be revised from time to time through boys leaving, I knew that in due course, I would be promoted to another task, and when it came a few months later, I found myself in the company of another boy, dusting, brushing and cleaning out the woodwork shop.

Another promotion I had in July was up to Form IV along with most of my classmates to be taught for the next twelve months by Mr Scott, whose main subject was French. He was an excellent teacher who had permission to teach Pitman shorthand in spare sessions, but to his form only. At the end of a few months under him, I felt my learning had improved tremendously. I liked the

French lessons and did well in the exams. I enjoyed too his teaching of shorthand, for which subject Mr Scott entered about a dozen of us for an 'outside' examination in which we all did well and each won a first class elementary shorthand certificate.

We were all devastated when Mr Scott dropped what must have been a bombshell to the governors, the Head and staff, when he gave notice of leaving for a higher post somewhere in the Lake District, and it was only after he had departed that we realised the School had lost an excellent master. Our new French master, when he arrived soon afterwards, was called Mr Lock. As it turned out, he knew German as well, and with permission he began to teach it to our class, so that although the shorthand went out of the window, a new language came in instead.

Mr Lock did not stay very long. He began a courtship with one of the resident mistresses from the girls' side and in next to no time both left to marry and move on to pastures new.

Mr Chapman succeeded Mr Lock as our form – and French – master. he too, was very good and became very popular with the boys. Between 1925 and 1927 we had a complete change of teachers apart from Mr Chynoweth and Mrs Jones. Mr Morgan was replaced by Mr Bond; Mr Williams by Mr Watcyn – another Welshman who went on to become Headmaster in later years. Mr Humphreys left and was replaced by Mr Pearson, who I must say, made a terrific improvement to the woodwork shop, both materially and practically. Mr HC Hughes, who had been Headmaster for six years, passed away on the School premises towards the end of 1926, after a short illness. He was very sadly missed by everyone.

Our new Headmaster arrived early in 1927 and his name was the Reverend R Bruce Wilson, who was married with three children, Ronald, Helen and another girl whose name I'm ashamed to say I cannot remember. The family was too large to take over the previous Headmaster's quarters in the School and were found residence in a house very close to the School.

I remember the house very well as I had an early introduction to it. By this time, my friend Alf and I were working together cleaning the dormitories, but we were detailed, along with two other workers, to go over one Saturday to help the new Head's wife clean the house and our expertise no doubt surprised and pleased her. It was a welcome change for us and we were apparently a great help to Mrs Wilson who insisted on giving us a little money "to put in the School bank" as we were not really allowed to keep money in our possession.

She also supplied us with sandwiches, cake and real tea with sugar in, which we drank out of real china cups. The Rev. Bruce Wilson was to remain head for the rest of my days at the School and continued to do so until 1944.

Before Mr Hughes had died I was in the top form and had been confirmed. It was a ritual every Monday that Mr Chynoweth ('Shinny') detailed four or five boys to learn by heart a passage from the Bible, to be recited by one of them in the Shirley Hall service the following Sunday afternoon.

I was detailed in due course and the next few days were spent reading and remembering at every spare moment. The passage I had to learn was part of the fourteenth chapter of St John's gospel. By the next Sunday morning, two of the boys had been selected by Shinny, and I was one. We both had to repair to the office at two o'clock for one only to be selected by the Head. To my surprise I was chosen and as I left the office it was with a thumping heart that I realised that in an hour or so I would be standing in the middle of the Shirley Hall with the boys and girls behind me and a couple of hundred strange faces in front of me, all listening to my young boyish voice reciting the second lesson.

I was very nervous and I passed two girls waiting to go into the office for the Head to choose one of them to recite the first lesson from the Old Testament. It was a tradition and rule that the boy who recited the lesson automatically became the gate boy for the following week.

His duty commenced at nine o'clock on Monday morning by reporting to Mr Harling in the School office, he doing secretarial work there as well as being organist and band master. The gate boy missed classes for the whole week and while on duty he sat on a chair placed just inside the main front doors, ready to answer the doorbell when it rang. His other duties entailed running little errands about the School for the Head, and occasionally going along the road to the shop at penny Lane corner and answering the telephone in the absence of others.

The old-fashioned telephone was perched high up on the office wall and even by standing on the one rung stool provided, I was so small I could not reach up. So the Head asked Mr Pearson, the new woodwork teacher to make a three rung stool just for me.

The gate boy's duties lasted all day until seven-thirty, being relieved only twice, once at twelve-thirty for dinner and again at five-thirty for tea. Answering the door bell was the most interesting as well as the most rewarding. Business visitors, Trustees, lady committee members etc, all sought interviews with the Head or the Matron, and were kind enough to tip the gate boy on their way out. Saturday was the best financially, when loads of visitors came with their parcels of fruit.

Money received during the day was taken from the gate boy each evening and dropped through a slit in Mr Harling's desk into a money box underneath. Then, on Monday morning at nine o'clock when the gate boy went off-duty, Mr Harling opened the desk and counted out the weekly tips. It averaged out from about ten shillings perhaps up to thirty on a good week. The gate boy was given half to put in his School bank book and the other half was given to the girl who had recited the lesson the Sunday before, for her to do likewise.

15
The Rest Of My School Days

I have not mentioned the School library. I had never seen it, but then neither had the majority of the other boys. A list of books held in the library was kept in the top form room. Every Monday a sheet of foolscap was passed around the classroom with the list of books and we added our name on the foolscap sheet together with the book we would like to borrow.

Two senior big boys were detailed to collect the books loaned out the previous week, take them back to the library and bring back the books required this week, and give them out. Often they would come back and say, "sorry, the book you require is not available so I've brought you this instead". It might be a copy of Pilgrim's Progress, the Bible, a big dictionary or the 'Way of Salvation' or some other religious publication. We were expected to take it all as a huge joke.

One day when I was on gate duty, there was a ring on the door bell and when I answered it I found an old blue on the step who I'll call Dixon to save any possible embarrassment, who had left the School a few months before. "I've come to see the Headmaster", he said. I brought him in and told him to wait, then I knocked on the door of the office which was at least always half open – the Head liked it that way – and I said, "Sir, Dixon, who left a short while ago, would like to speak to you".

"Ask him to wait a moment", he replied. Then after a couple of minutes the Head shouted, "Come in, Dixon". Then as Dixon went in I heard the Head say, "leave that door open – now, Dixon, what can I do for you?"

I did not have to ear-wig but I heard every word of the conversation.

"Well, sir", began Dixon, "that job I got when I left school has turned out to be very poor. Not much money, no hope of promotion for ages and the prospects look dismal. A friend of mine told me there is plenty of scope for better things in Australia with the help of the Salvation Army, so I made enquiries and they can help me out and even pay my passage to Australia – but first they want a reference from you. Can you please give me one, Sir?"

There was a silence for a few seconds, then I heard the Head say, "Oh, so you're going to emigrate?"

"No, Sir!" came the quick reply from Dixon, "I'm going to Australia, I told you so before."

Dixon was told to wait, but the Head changed his mind and said, "Let me have your address quickly and I will post a reference on to you."

I said goodbye and good luck to Dixon on the way out, but I never heard of him again.

I felt I knew what emigrating meant, but thought to be on the safe side I would look in that large dictionary in the library for confirmation. So, when my relief came for tea, instead of going to the dining hall in the usual way, I decided to go through the Shirley Hall and find the library on the way. I practically tip-toed through the Shirley Hall, opened the door on the far side very quietly and tip-toed down a flight of wooden stairs. I was about to tip-toe up a flight of stairs opposite them when I nearly jumped out of my skin when a loud voice shouted, "And where do you think you are going, Ross?"

I looked round into the shadows and saw it was the Matron creeping about as usual in her rubber-soled shoes. "The library, matron," I replied. Then she said, "You should know as well as I do that this part of the building is out of bounds to you" and then with what I thought sounded like a note of triumph in her voice added, "besides, the library will be locked – so hurry down quickly or you will miss your tea."

I never did find out where the library was located.

It was in the summer of 1927 when one day sitting chatting on the bank of the School yard with a group of friends, one of them drew from his pocket a small book he had borrowed. It was a book on fortune-telling, giving various illustrations, one of which was the drawing of a human hand showing all the different lines such as the heart and life lines etc.

We had a lot of fun comparing our own hands and lines with the drawing, and telling each other nonsensical fortunes, but it was noticed that one friend of mine, Charles Saggers, who was eleven years old at the time, had an exceptionally short life line. He was able to see it too and in our stupid boyish way we ragged him about it, which as it happened did not upset him at all and he took it in good fun.

A couple of weeks later we went home for our September holiday. My sister and I, together with Charlie and his sister Doris, sat on the front outside seat on the top of a number four tramcar on the way home, while our mothers sat downstairs. The tram stopped at Holy Trinity Church next to the School where a funeral was taking place. There was a very large gathering of mourners attending, and as we watched, Charlie said for seemingly no reason at all. "I suppose there would be a big crowd like that at my funeral, wouldn't there?"

Doris said, "Don't be silly, Charlie, you're not going to die yet. You are too young."

I could no help thinking back to that fortune-telling book and Charlie's short life line, but I remained silent. The following

Sunday morning, my sister and I had gone to our local church at home, and when we got back a visitor had just arrived. He was Charlie's elder brother and my mother was in tears.

We were told then that Charlie had gone to spend a few days in a bungalow in North Wales with older sisters only the day before. Apparently he had volunteered to carry fresh water from a standpipe nearby. He was on his way back with a bucket of water when he hurried out from behind a hedge and into the path of a bus. He died immediately from his injuries.

We were devastated by the sad news, and again my thoughts flew back to that fortune-telling book. Obviously only co-incidental but how very true. The tragedy was reported in the local papers and as Charlie had supposed there was indeed a very large crowd at his funeral later that week.

The burial service was held in that same Holy Trinity church and was attended by well over one hundred boys and girls from the School. His coffin was borne by six big boys from the School, and Charlie was laid to rest in Holy Trinity churchyard, only a couple of hundred yards in a straight line from the spot on the bank where we had studied the fortune-telling book.

Our September holiday was a very sad affair, and going back to School was dismal having to experience the emptiness of a missing friend. Life however, had to go on for us, so we buckled down to the new long term and had to make the most of it. I soon got the chance to play for the School's first eleven. I possessed a football or caseball as we called them in those days. It had been bought for me by an uncle, and one day our House monitor, Jim Hitchmough, asked if he could borrow it to enable our Shirley House team practice for a forthcoming House match.

He told me I could practice with them as it was my ball. How very kind, I though sarcastically, but I did lend them my ball and played with them. I found I could more than hold my own playing in the forward line, and I was pleased to play a few more games with them. When the match day came, one player had gone 'up in knock' and so they were one player short. Jim Hitchmough asked me to make up the eleven and I was very happy to oblige.

I had a good game, which brought me to the notice of Shinny, the sports master. He, to my surprise and delight, introduced me into the first team and I played outside right. I was quite small as lads go, but I could run fast and from then on I never looked back and I was glad I had loaned out my ball when I did.

It was grand playing away-games. Some took us on a long bus or tram ride around the town in Saturday afternoons, and Shinny often bought us packets of sweets as a special treat, and was always there at half-time with the oranges.

I will always remember one game we played away. It was against the boys from the Able Seaman's training ship, *Indefatigable*, anchored in the Mersey. We went by tram to the Pier Head and then by ferry across the River to New Ferry on the Wirral, thence by bus to the ground. We met the opposition at the ground which was flooded as it had been raining for hours.

We were surprised when the *Indefatigable* boys came onto the pitch, they were much older and certainly much bigger and heavier. Although we did give them a good game, they knocked the stuffing out of us and we lost three to one. I must place on record that it was the only game we lost during my two and half seasons playing for the Blue Coat.

After the game we went back to the ferry with the opposition as we had been invited on board their training ship. We were met at the ferry by a large rowing boat onto which we all clambered and four big strapping lads rowed us to their ship at anchor in the middle of the river. A companionway was slung over the ship's side for us to climb aboard and we were piped onto the deck and taken below.

By this time it was almost dark outside but the ship was well lit up and seemed warm and cosy. Being led to a cabin where we could drop our kit, a whistle blew and everyone around including us had to stop dead in our tracks for about half a minute and stand to attention until the whistle was blown again. We were told this was done for disciplinarian reasons and, indeed, although we were only on board for an hour and a half the whistle was blown a number of times.

After being shown around the ship, we were led into the mess, where a special table had been laid for us. A plate of sandwiches and cakes were laid before us and instead of a teacup a basin was provided. One of the cooks came from the galley and filled each basin with so called tea which was not very palatable and one or two of our number were able to pour the tea out through a porthole nearby.

We were surprised to see the lower ranks on the ship running about in bare feet with their trousers rolled up to their knees. Meanwhile Mr Chynoweth had been taken to the Officers' mess and by all accounts fared only a little better than we did. Altogether it was a wonderful experience and as we were rowed back to New Ferry we gave them three hearty cheers from our rowing boat while they all lined the decks of the *Indefatigable* and waved us their goodbyes.

We were hoping for a return match, but it never materialised.

16
The End In Sight

I may have mentioned earlier that for our May and September holidays we always by tradition were let out of School at eight o'clock on a Monday morning. For the first time in living memory this was changed to a Saturday commencing with the May holiday in 1928.

At first we wondered why and thought perhaps the Governors were being extra kind to us, but we were eventually given to understand it was to satisfy the constant demands of the resident teachers who had wanted an extra weekend at their homes. We were inclined to forget they too were bound by the same rules and regulations and timewise they must have suffered like us. I remember one master telling us one time that he would have had more Christmases at home if he had joined the Navy instead of the Blue Coat.

So on Saturday the 5th May 1928 we started our holiday and it was a special day for any Blue Coat Evertonians, as Everton were playing their final fixture against Arsenal at Goodison Park. Dixie Dean had already scored fifty seven league goals that season. Could he make it sixty and create a new record?

A large number of Blue Coat Evertonians agreed to meet outside Goodison at two o'clock and we all queued for and gained entry to the boys' pen. I made sure my friend Alf came with me, as he had never seen a professional game of football and I don't suppose he ever saw another as he was not really interested. We saw the game which ended in a three all draw and Dixie netted the three goals he needed and created that footballing record that has never been broken, and because we Blue Coat boys had been let out on the Saturday instead of the Monday, we were witnesses.

Back from our May holiday we soon settled down to face the short summer term, and prepare ourselves for the exams etc. During the holiday the Catechist had found himself a job and had left the School. The Headmaster chose me to replace him, and from then on my Sundays would be a little different. There were two final rehearsals after dinner, one for the boys and one for the girls, the latter meant I had to go over to the girls' side about two o'clock and in the presence of the senior mistress and the Matron in a classroom I asked the girls their questions and received their answers which were from memory. I held the book and could correct them if they slipped up, but I very seldom needed to, they were all so good.

For the afternoon service my job was to hand out hynnbooks to the visitors coming into Shirley Hall and then during the service standing by the Headmaster until time for the questions and answers on the Catechism. I continued with this position of Catechist until I was to leave some ten months later.

Alf was still bringing back the latest song sheets and singing the songs to us and playing them on his mouth organ. He also liked to play-act stories from comics and having some of us act them out. He often toyed with the idea of forming his own jazz band telling us that Rushworths the music furnishers frequently had sales, and second-hand drum-kits could be had for as little as half a guinea, and other second-hand instruments from about seven shillings and sixpence up. In his mind's eye he saw himself on the drums, me on the trumpet and another pal on the trombone etc. Where the money was to come from he had no idea and he suggested we should start saving up. We used to wonder from where he got all this show biz interest, but even with all his enthusiasm he never got any further.

By now it was the summer of 1928 and I had been in the School for four years and I felt reminded of what an older boy had told me in my early days that nothing changes, one year is like the next, and I realised what stereotyped lives we were all leading. Two of my younger brothers had been admitted into the School as they came of age, Jim in 1926 and Alec two years later, and we were naturally some little source of comfort and companionship to each other. There was one noticeable feature, however, that as we grew older the familiar faces of our contemporaries were fast disappearing as jobs were found for them and they left to start new lives working for a living.

So it was that in this summer of 1928 there was another revision in the workers' list, and Alf and I were promoted to senior workers, i.e. the 'stayers out', which meant we would be staying out of class in the mornings of alternate weeks, and this new job was to last us both until the end of our school-days, and we scrubbed and polished and carried out our tasks very well. Had there been any 'A' levels in those days I am sure we would have been awarded A+ in brushing, dusting, polishing and scrubbing.

Alf and I spent hours and hours together at work, and naturally we talked a lot between ourselves and occasionally, as we thought of the future he might say, "Just imagine, ten years from now we could be courting," and I would reply, "perhaps even married," to which he would reply, "yes, even with children!" The thoughts were frightening at the time, but little did we know that in a little over ten years from then, I would be a member of the Auxiliary Air Force at Speke, and he going away to sea in the Merchant Navy.

As it turned out, Alf was to marry before me and his wife bore him a son who was christened John who grew up to be a fine boy, and by the time he was twenty was becoming world famous, and so just for the record, that baby boy of Alf's was none other than John Lennon. It has always intrigued me that while the show biz in Alf never blossomed, it flourished and materialised in his son.

Christmas 1928 was to be our last in the Blue Coat, and as it turned out was the last Christmas the children spent in the School, for the following year, a two hundred years or so tradition was broken when the children were allowed a fortnight's holiday in their own homes. Early in 1929, Alf left the School and I followed him out a couple of months later.

When we left we were kitted out as indeed all the boys were, with a new suit, a couple of striped flannel shirts, two stiff collars, studs and a tie, two pairs of socks, one pair of boots and a bowler hat. Whether one was going to be an apprenticed plumber, or away to sea or to an office job, all were given a bowler hat.

During the morning I was leaving, I was going around saying my goodbyes when I met Nurse Taylor in the corridor. I was dressed in my new civilian clothes and she asked, "Are you coming to see me, Ross?"

I replied, "Yes Nurse, in about quarter of an hour."

"Good," she said, "I'll have a dose of gregory powder ready for you".

She was only joking of course, but she was renowned for administering doses of gregory powder, especially to boys who she thought were malingering when reporting sick. 'Greg' as we called it was her not so secret weapon, and one teaspoonful mixed in half a cup of cold water was really horrid and was by far the worst tasting medicine any of us had ever experienced. It was officially given to us all as opening medicine at lease twice a year and we all loathed it.

Nurse wished me good luck for the future and appeared grateful as I thanked her for the attention she had afforded me over the years. I carried on saying my goodbyes, and finally sought out my brothers Jim and Alec whom I was sorry to be leaving behind. I was allowed to go over to the girls' side and say goodbye to my sister Mary whom I left in tears. They were naturally upset at my departing and I never could describe the sadness I felt, not just at leaving them, but at leaving the place which had been my home for almost five years.

The Headmaster, the Rev. Bruce Wilson, walked with me from his office out onto the front steps, and as he shook my hand and wished me goodbye and good luck, he handed me my school reference which I still treasure. I walked briskly down the path with my case in one hand, holding onto my bowler hat with the other as there was quite a stiff breeze blowing.

As I reached the tall iron gates and walked off the School premises, I looked back over my shoulder and the memories crowded in, both happy and sad, and had I realised then what I have realised since, I must surely have said to myself, "Thank God for the Blue Coat School".

Also available from Pharaoh Press

Memoirs of a Liverpool Stripper

by Flo Jones *ISBN 0 95255431 3*

Florence Louise Titherington was born in Anfield, Liverpool, in 1910. Her story takes us from the first sight of Germans in World War I through her childhood years until the start of World War II. It is a compelling tale of life as it really was, with all its hardships, seen through the eyes of a child.

Price £4.99

Haunted Liverpool

by Thomas Slemen *ISBN 0 9525543 3 X*

According to the Guinness Book of Records, Britain has more ghosts than any other country in the world, and it seems Liverpool has more than its fair share! In Haunted Liverpool, Thomas Slemen takes you on a chilling tour of the city's haunted sites. Read on if you dare ...

Price £5.99

Journey of Awareness

by Christina O'Sullivan

"I hope this book will help you understand a little more about head injury and what it means to the people who live with it day after day."

Price £3.50

Pier Head Jump

by Tommy Miller

ISBN 0 9525543 4 8

His Co-Op bicycle still on the quay-side, the young Tommy Miller looks on in horror as the gangway is raised. Suddenly he is leaving his beloved Liverpool. And he only boarded the Empire McDermott to get some ciggies! Tommy's adventures have taken him from Liverpool to the four corners of the world, and back again. Will he find anyone who likes scousers? Will he find a change of clothes? Will the Co-Op get their bike back? Read on ...

Price £5.99

Kiss of the Lion

by Susan E Westoby

ISBN 0 9522253 2 1

As the French army swept through Italy like an irresistible tide, bearing all before it, Valentina Velucci found herself sold in marriage to the most powerful of the French Lords, Raoul de Baisleon, the 'Lion of France'. Trapped in a deadly game of intrigue and betrayal, fiercely desired by Cesare Borgia, the dark and ruthless son of Pope Alexander, Valentina was forced to give herself into his power to save her husband from a traitor's death.

Caught between the passion of two men who would stop at nothing to possess her, Valentina fought for the love she valued more than anything – even life itself.

Price £5.99

Brave Heart

by Susan E Westoby

ISBN 0 9525543 0 5

Beaten, raped and abused. Elenor de Beauvrais barely survived the horror of her marriage to Gerard, Lord of Fernrean. There seemed to be no escape from an existence of degradation and pain – until the day she overheard her husband's plot to ambush King William.

Armand de Carrefour, bodyguard to the king. A hard man, yet supremely honourable. William sent him to protect the Lady de Beauvrais, but could he ignore the dictates of his warrior's heart?

Price £5.99

Saxon Falcon

by Susan E Westoby

ISBN 0 903348 47 0

He was her enemy – yet his love and desire lit a flame in her heart which consumed her body and soul. Edith of Sensgarth was a prize for which the Norman Lord, Michel du Formeils was finally prepared to give up all he possessed. Saer de Friese coveted Michel's lands and power – but when he stole his wife, he signed his own death warrant.

Price £4.95